THE MAN, THE CHARACTER, THE LEGEND

DEANMANIA

ROBERT HEADRICK, JR.

PIONEER BOOKS LAS VEGAS

OTHER PIONEER BOOKS

•FISTS OF FURY: THE FILMS OF BRUCE LEE
Written by Edward Gross. March, 1990. $14.95, ISBN #1-55698-233-X
•WHO WAS THAT MASKED MAN?
Written by James Van Hise. March, 1990. $14.95, ISBN #1-55698-227-5
•PAUL MCCARTNEY: 20 YEARS ON HIS OWN
Written by Edward Gross. February, 1990. $9.95, ISBN #1-55698-263-1
•THE DARK SHADOWS TRIBUTE BOOK
Written by Edward Gross and James Van Hise. February, 1990. $14.95, ISBN#1-55698-234-8
•THE UNOFFICIAL TALE OF BEAUTY AND THE BEAST, 2nd Edition
Written by Edward Gross. $14.95, 164 pages, ISBN #1-55698-261-5
•TREK: THE LOST YEARS
Written by Edward Gross. $12.95, 128 pages, ISBN #1-55698-220-8
•THE TREK ENCYCLOPEDIA
Written by John Peel. $19.95, 368 pages, ISBN#1-55698-205-4
•HOW TO DRAW ART FOR COMIC BOOKS
Written by James Van Hise. $14.95, 160 pages, ISBN#1-55698-254-2
•THE TREK CREW BOOK
Written by James Van Hise. $9.95, 112 pages, ISBN#1-55698-256-9
•THE DOCTOR AND THE ENTERPRISE
Written by Jean Airey. $9.95, 136 pages, ISBN#1-55698-218-6
•THE MAKING OF THE NEXT GENERATION
Written by Edward Gross. $14.95, 128 pages, ISBN#1-55698-219-4
•BATMANIA
Written by James Van Hise. $14.95, 176 pages, ISBN#1-55698-252-6
•GUNSMOKE
Written by John Peel. $14.95, 204 pages, ISBN#1-55698-221-6
•ELVIS-THE MOVIES: THE MAGIC LIVES ON
Written by Hal Schuster. $14.95, ISBN#1-55698-223-2
•STILL ODD AFTER ALL THESE YEARS: ODD COUPLE COMPANION.
Written by Edward Gross. $12.95, 132 pages, ISBN#1-55698-224-0
•SECRET FILE: THE UNOFFICIAL MAKING OF A WISEGUY
Written by Edward Gross. $14.95, 164 pages, ISBN#1-55698-261-5
•THE SECRET OF MICHAEL J FOX'S SUCCESS
Written by Edward Gross. $14.95
•THE FILMS OF EDDIE MURPHY
Written by Edward Gross. $14.95

Designed and Edited by Hal Schuster

Library of Congress Cataloging-in-Publication Data
Robert J. Headrick, Jr.—
DEANMANIA: The Man, The Character, The Legend

1. DEANMANIA: The Man, The Character, The Legend (film)
I. Title

Published by Pioneer Books, Inc., 5715 N. Balsam Rd., Las Vegas, NV, 89130.

First Printing, 1990

Dedication
This book is dedicated to Mom, Dad, Beth, Chuck, Haley, Aaron, and Hilary; they are the GIANTS in my life. Without them, I too might be a "REBEL WITHOUT A CAUSE"...

Acknowledgements

To write a book such as DEANMANIA required the assistance of many people. To begin with there are the dozens and dozens of "We Remember Dean International" fans who wrote me and provided me with encouragement, responses to my probing questions, and many, many photographs. I am equally thankful for the many statements (some included in DEANMANIA) made by James Dean fans during the last 10 years, many of which were gleaned from past issues of the "We Remember Dean International" newsletters. Readers will find remarks made by many of these fans throughout the section detailing fans and their recollections of James Dean. I am sorry not to include remarks and photographs sent by each fan, but to do so would have greatly increased the present size of the book. It should however be very clear to any reader of this book that the dedication of James Dean's fans is one of the single greatest contributions to his continued popularity now thirty-five years after his death. Thanks to each of you!

A very special thanks must also be extended to two people very instrumental in my writing this book. You would not be holding a copy of DEANMANIA if it were not for Sylvia Bongiovanni and Bob Pulley. The extent to which each of these persons was willing to help me at times when many others seemed less than interested or unavailable for assistance will never be forgotten. Sylvia and Bob are truly remarkable people, and their dedication to the perpetuation of the spirit and memory of James Dean is without equal. Thank you both very much!!!!

A big thanks must be given to special friends who put up with my obsession for James Dean—to Denny and Kathy Hill (my photographer extraordinaire and his patient wife) and the newest little Hill (who by now has no doubt been named); and to Jeff and Traci Coons and to Don and Joyce Gordy (friends who are always on the look-out for new Dean items).

A special thanks to Robert Rees, Maxine Rowland, Tom Marshall, David Loehr, and the many others who sent information with respect to Dean collectibles—I wish it were possible to publish each and every photograph sent. Thanks too, to Enrico Perego for the photography of his collection, and more importantly, for allowing me to share it with you, the readers.

Thanks to Gayla at Film Favorites, finding just the right illustrative materials became a pleasure. Thanks to Hal Schuster, editor and publisher, for believing in this project.

I know that there are people who helped with this project during its development, which now approaches a year in length, whom I have unintentionally omitted. I am sorry.

Finally, you the readers, now have the task of evaluating the extent to which I have accomplished my goal. It should be noted that any deficiencies are entirely my own and not of the people recognized here. Should you feel inclined to do so, please drop me a line in care of my publisher. I'd love to hear from you.

—Robert J. Headrick, Jr.

June, 1990

Preface

In DEANMANIA I have tried to be as complete and accurate as possible. However, I discovered as I wrote the book that there was a great deal more to explore and write about than I had earlier imagined. I reached a point where I had to refuse to expand the present work. Suffice it to say that DEANMANIA only begins to explore the MAN, CHARACTER, and LEGEND of JAMES DEAN. My sincerest hope is that DEANMANIA will provide fans with an entertaining work which details, in both text and photography, the career of one of America's truly great cinema stars. There will no doubt be a few unintentional omissions and errors. For each of these I apologize. What became very evident to me as I researched the life and career of James Dean was that there are many facets of his life that have been interpreted in as many ways as there are persons to interpret them. It is unfortunate that so much of this misinterpretation has skewed our understanding of James Dean. However, because the great majority of Dean's fans refuse to believe everything they read, James Dean has escaped being the victim of many overzealous writers—many of whom simply don't have their facts straight.

As David Dalton alludes to in his JAMES DEAN THE MUTANT KING, there is indeed a James Dean myth—to those who knew him, he seems very real—to those of us who did not know him, he seems almost greater than life itself—perhaps for those who question his very existence DEANMANIA THE MAN, THE CHARACTER, THE LEGEND will shed some light.

For those who are not already devoted James Dean fans, if you become hooked and want to learn more about James Dean, you might consider joining the "We Remember Dean International" fan club. The address is:

We Remember Dean International Club
Post Office Box 5025
Fullerton, California 92635

I hope you enjoy DEANMANIA.

Contents

M. CALLAHAN
JOAN JONES
CLYMER
VA JEAN REYNOLDS
JAMES B. DEAN
ELENOR

PART ONE
James Dean: The Man

"If a man can bridge the gap between life and death. I mean, if he can live on after he's died, then he was a great man." —James Dean

Who is James Dean?

"James Dean milked cows, tended chickens, drove a tractor, raised a bull, played star basketball, studied yoga and the clarinet, learned something about almost every field of knowledge, and finally became what in the modern world incarnates the myth of total life, a movie star."

—The Case of James Dean, Edgar Morin

Who is James Dean? James Byron Dean was born to Winton and Mildred (Wilson) Dean on February 8, 1931, at Green Gables Apartments on East Fourth Street in Marion, Indiana.

Today, many people consider James Dean a phenomenon. To three generations he has become an icon, whose stature and reputation is squarely balanced upon three films he completed before his tragic death in September, 1955. There is no question that Dean's life, every facet of it, has been fully explored and exploited by both those faithful to his memory, and those who are curious. The amount of documentation about James Dean that has been committed to writing leaves little doubt as to his popularity and his status as the perennial "first American teenager".

For many Dean was a teenage symbol of the 1950s. The 1950s youth generation saw in him a reflection of themselves—never before had a single individual so dramatically portrayed teenage frustrations. He was intense, lonely, frustrated, angry, sullen and uncompromising and for most of the youth at this time he became the archetypal rebel for every cause. He was the "first American teenager" and although he has been dead now for thirty-five years, he remains for many the "perennial teenager."

David Considine, in THE CINEMA OF ADOLESCENCE, suggests that "Dean...whether as Cal or Jim, and even later as Jett in GIANT, suggested the vulnerability of adolescence. His appeal was in part a result of his own nature and a result of human nature. As a rebel in all three films [EAST OF EDEN, REBEL WITHOUT A CAUSE, and GIANT], he established an image that still remains..." It is this very image that has for the last 35 years defied definition.

To answer the question, "Who is James Dean?" it seems only appropriate to examine what Dean's friends have said about him.

Traces
of Indiana and Midwestern History
Fall 1989 Vol. 1, No. 4 A Publication of the Indiana Historical Society $5.00
JAMES DEAN'S INDIANA
GRANT COUNTY'S OWN
TRAVELING BROWN COUNTY
GROWING UP WITH COLE PORTER

Dean's early friends included Barbara Glenn, Bill Gun, Bill Bast, Martin Landau, Dennis Hopper, Sal Mineo, Vampira, and others. What seems very striking about each of his friends is that no two of them ever described Jim in quite the same fashion. The disharmony that occurs among Dean's friends when asked to describe him attests to the depth of his persona. Answers provided by a few of his friends as well as several people with whom he worked, will provide one dimension to this multi-dimensional character. Thus in order to fully answer the question, "Who is James Dean?" we must probe deeper.

A second group of people to whom we pose this same question are the many fans who for the past 35 years have perpetuated his spirit and memory. Their answers are just as varied and they too provide yet another dimension to James Dean. In many instances their answers approach an almost idolatrous status. What seems obvious, nevertheless, is that for many fans, there are specific traits, characteristics, and mannerisms of James Dean in the characters he created on film—Cal Trask, Jim Stark, and Jett Rink that attract them to him. To many of these fans it appears difficult to determine where the characters end and Dean begins. The extent to which fans have memorialized him for the past three decades attests to their dedication to keeping his memory alive.

Perhaps the most personal, and in many ways, the most correct answer to the question, "Who is James Dean?" will be found with remarks by Bob Pulley, a classmate of James Dean. It seems only fitting that such a friend could provide us with perceptions that were developed long before James Dean became something more than a "young man from Fairmount, Indiana." It is obvious from Bob's comments that there was indeed a James Dean that we don't know—one that according to the people who knew him in Fairmount was not a symbol of rebellion and defiance.

In a recent feature in TRACES magazine, Jim's aunt Ortense Winslow (who raised Jim in Fairmount) provides us with a picture of James Dean that is very unlike what many have been lead to believe: "He was talented. He was born that way. He wasn't ornery, but you always knew he was around, if you know what I mean. Those things they say about him and what he was like just make me angry because I know they aren't true." In this same article, his uncle Marcus Winslow further asserts that "[h]e was like all boys his age. He wasn't perfect, and he got into his share of trouble. He was raised decent, but they say he was ill-mannered and ill-bred, and I don't understand that."

No matter how much Jim has suffered at the hands of writers and reporters through the years, it appears that each group of persons included here — friends, fans, or family — found something about him that has contributed to the creation of James Dean, the man.

While James Dean speaks to us in each of his movies, it seems only fitting that he should have at least an opportunity to speak about himself directly. Throughout this book readers will find many things that Dean himself said at one time or another during his short life. While James Dean didn't have the opportunity to write an autobiography—it seems unlikely that he would have done so even if he could—he did nevertheless provide us with a short piece that describes his early life. This piece was a school assignment, and it is included here because it clearly demonstrates the extent to which Jim was like most any other teenager (he wrote it when he was 17) and yet, it also indicates an awareness Jim held for the establishment of goals in life and the accomplishment of them.

On September 30, 1960 James Dean was memorialized at Fairmount High School, Fairmount Indiana. Parts of the text of the memorial service are included here because they demonstrate further the extent to which impressions of James Dean are important to us.

Each of these groups of people provides answers that are based upon different recollections and memories of James Dean. What these people have to say provides us a beginning from which to explore the first dimension of James Dean, JAMES DEAN THE MAN.

James Dean, "My Case Study"

In 1948, when James Dean was seventeen years old, a new principal came to Fairmount High School. The new principal, Roland Dubois, asked each of the students to write a short autobiography in order to help him get to know each one better. James Dean wrote the following which he titled, "My Case Study."

My Case Study by James Dean

I, James Byron Dean was born February 8, 1931, Marion Indiana. My parents, Winton Dean and Mildred Dean formerly Mildred Wilson, and myself existed in the state of Indiana until I was six years of age.

Dad's work with the government caused a change so Dad as a dental mechanic was transferred to California. There we lived until the fourth year. Mom became ill and passed out of my life at the age of nine. I never knew the reason for mom's death, in fact it still preys on my mind.

I had always lived such a talented life. I studied violin, played in concerts, tap-danced on theatre stages but most of all I like art, to mold and create things with my hands.

I came back to Indiana to live with my uncle. I lost the dancing and violin but not the art. I think my life will be devoted to art and dramatics. And there are so many different fields of art it would be hard to foul up, and if I did there are so many different things to do—farm, sports, science, geology, coaching, teaching, music. I got it and I know if I better myself then there will be no match. A fellow must have confidence.

When living in California my young eyes experienced many things. It was also my luck to make three visiting trips to Indiana, going and coming a different route each time. I have been in almost every state west of Indiana, I remember all.

My hobby, or what I do in my spare time, is motorcycle. I know a lot about them mechanically and I love to ride. I have been in a few races and I have done well. I own a small cycle myself. When I'm not doing that I'm usually engaged in athletics, the heartbeat of every American boy. As one strives to make a goal in life in a game there should be a goal in this crazy world for each of us. I hope I know what mine is, anyway, I'm after it....

JAMES DEAN

courtesy Fairmount Historical Museum

Growing up with Jimmie

Bob Pulley today.

Courtesy Bob Pulley

Robert Pulley is not at all unlike many people who live in Fairmount, Indiana when it comes to being asked questions about James Dean. He is besieged by many James Dean fans when they first come to Fairmount. "They want to know everything and that's what got me started," he says.

Because of his friendship with James Dean, when both were young kids growing up together in Fairmount, he has a lot to tell. He does however admit that he, like a few others who also grew up with Jimmy Dean, hasn't always been willing to answer the many questions asked. As a matter of fact, he admits candidly, until about five years ago, he wasn't as accommodating as he is today.

Now, decades after his death, there remain a few close friends of Dean in Fairmount. They are reluctant to become involved in what has for Bob Pulley become almost a full-time job.

Robert Pulley is President of the Fairmount Historical Museum Board, whose duty it is to preserve the memorabilia associated with James Dean on public display in two rooms at the Fairmount Historical Museum.

James Dean isn't Fairmount's only famous son — CBS correspondent Phil Jones and the creator of Garfield, Jim Davis, are both Fairmount natives. Yet, according to Bob Pulley, "nine out of 10 want to know about Jim."

Although Bob Pulley is retired, it is obvious he hasn't slowed down enough to enjoy retirement. The amount of time he dedicates to the Fairmount Historical Society and to the many who want to probe deeply into his youth while growing up with James Dean occupy his time.

To visit with Bob Pulley is truly a pleasure. His frankness about his friend James Dean is both refreshing and enlightening. I found visiting with Bob the surest route to better understanding James Dean as a person.

It was clear from our visit that there is truly a side of James Dean that simply has not been discussed. While I wish I could share everything I learned about James Dean from Bob Pulley, I believe the answers provided by Bob will provide yet another facet to an increasingly difficult question to answer, "Who is James Dean?"

I began by asking Bob when he first met Jim. He recalled, "I suppose it must have been during some sort of sports competition. We went to different grade schools.

"Jimmy always wanted to be the best. He kept working at something until he got it. Like when us boys would be playin' a game of basketball and we'd stop for a break, and Jim would still be out there shootin'. He was no different than any other kid."

It is clear that James Dean was very much a product of his time. Bob elaborated, "Jimmy was just like any other boy and he wasn't a loner. He was just an ordinary person. He wasn't any different. A little mischievous.

"Many of his friends still live around here," he continued. "Yet they are reluctant to talk about him—not because they wouldn't say positive things, but rather because they are afraid of becoming so involved with all that has happened since his death.

"He wasn't (a rebel)—he wasn't moody as he often is portrayed."

"To me, and his friends, it was (always) Jim or Jimmy. James was Hollywood. But we also called him Dean or 'Deaner'."

Fans often speculate what would have become of James Dean if he hadn't turned to acting but instead stayed in Fairmount. So I asked Bob. He said, "I don't know what Jimmy would have done if he'd stayed in Fairmount. I do know this, he's sitting up there somewhere looking down on us—on this museum—and he's laughing at all those crazy people here making such a big fuss over him. He might have become a farmer.

"In 1955 when he came back home to visit—he was the same James Dean that had left. He did however, follow Stock's directions, when it came to posing for pictures. That was a little unlike Jim.

"The character and person in EAST OF EDEN are Jim. The character in REBEL and GIANT are not in my opinion James Dean.

"(The last time I saw Jim) was February, 1955. We got together and we partied—he hadn't changed a bit. We had a good time that night. At a bar in nearby Marion, he filled his mouth with lighter fluid, then sprayed the fluid through a lit match, sending a fire ball sailing through the air. A Fairmount man who happened to

Before Jim left in February 1955 he gave Bob Pulley his address in California and told him to come and visit him.

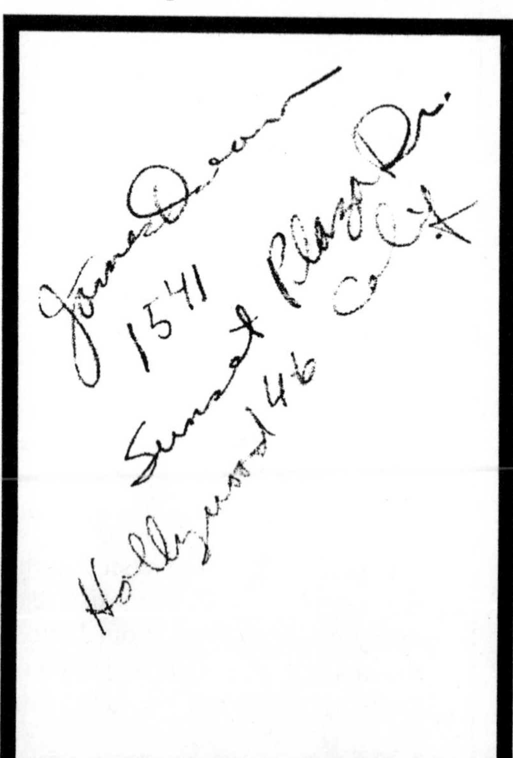

Courtesy of Bob Pulley

be in the bar asked him for his autograph, then tore it up in front of him. That really hurt Jim. I'll bet that guy wishes he had it today."

The legend of James Dean grew and grew after his death, yet no one knows how Dean would have reacted to it. Bob felt he was "up there right now laughing at all this stuff goin' on. He would have enjoyed it all—he was proud of himself—he would have taken part in all of the celebration that takes place here each fall."

Fairmount High School Track Team-front row, James Dean, far left and Bob Pulley, far right. Courtesy of Bob Pulley

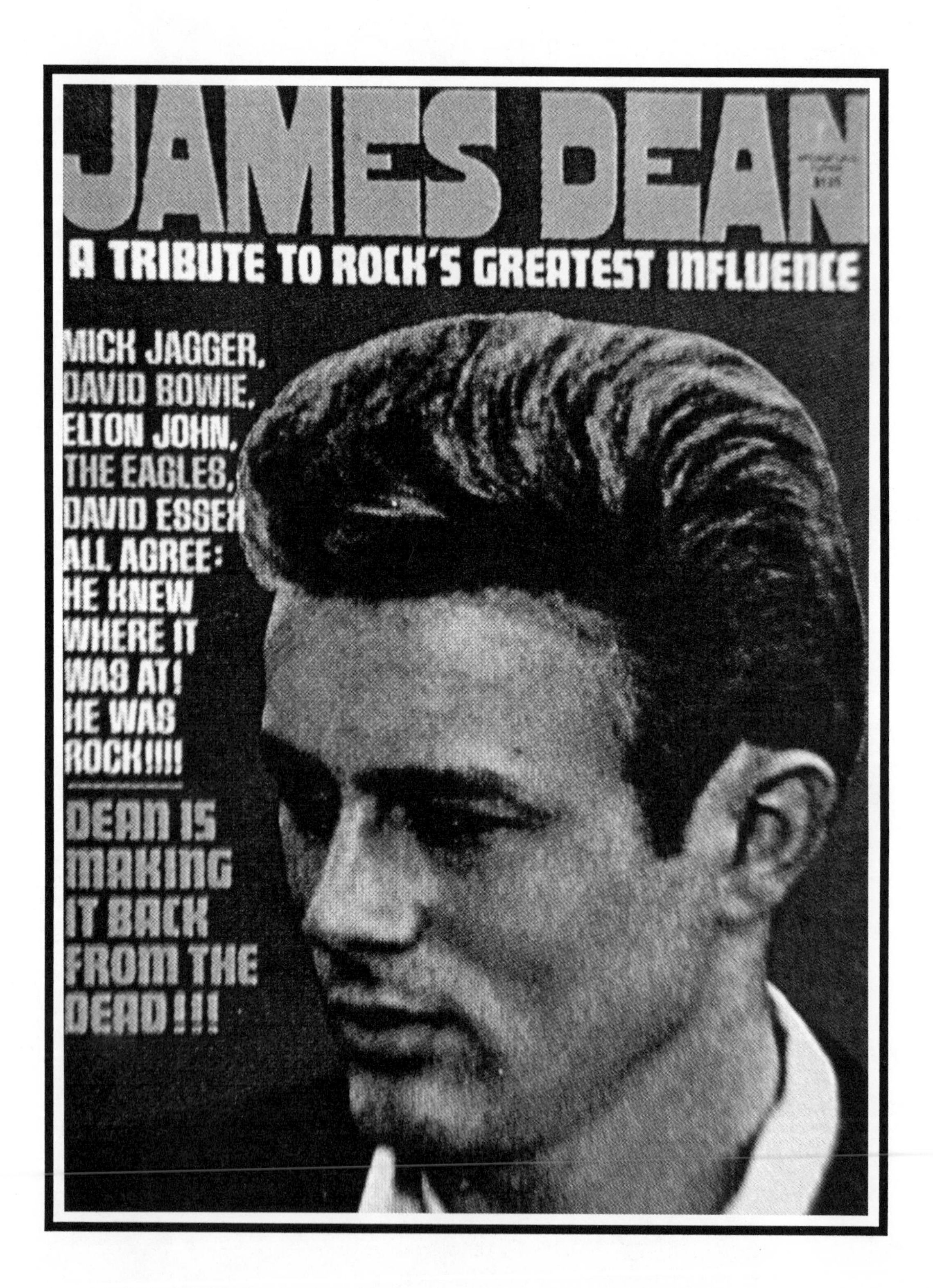
JAMES DEAN
A TRIBUTE TO ROCK'S GREATEST INFLUENCE
MICK JAGGER,
DAVID BOWIE,
ELTON JOHN,
THE EAGLES,
DAVID ESSEX
ALL AGREE:
HE KNEW
WHERE IT
WAS AT!
HE WAS
ROCK!!!!
DEAN IS
MAKING
IT BACK
FROM THE
DEAD!!!

Those who knew or worked with James Dean recall that...

"The few roles he played tended to create an image of him that was considerably off the mark."
—William Bast, JAMES DEAN A BIOGRAPHY

"He was a rebel without a cause for a generation of youth in search of a hero. Dean's sullen and uncompromising independence fired the imagination, giving the young a champion, who by his example would lead them out of the post-war rut."
—Ronald Martinetti, THE JAMES DEAN STORY

"At various times in his life Jimmy was hooked on: bongo drums, bullfighting, ballet, rude silence, incessant talk, loud music, drawing, sculpturing, piano playing, recorder tooting, practical jokes, sloppiness, exhaustion, ambition, or any of these in combination with his biggest high: acting...He was always pushing into new things, pushing into new people, hoping that something or someone would stop him, tell him his limits, tell him who he was. But he kept winning! And nobody tells a winner what to do."
—Venable Herndon, JAMES DEAN A SHORT LIFE

"James Dean was the strongest influence of any actor that ever stepped in front of the camera. Ever! And that strength has never really diminished. If anything, it has grown. Young people who weren't even alive at the time are still influenced by his work. That's the power of film when it's done that well—which is not very often."
—Martin Sheen

"[Jim was] a restless, enigmatic artist in a passionate search for fulfillment, a reckless youth in a fatal race with destiny."
—William Bast, JAMES DEAN A BIOGRAPHY

"Jimmy and I found we were a bit neurotic and had to justify our neurosis by creating, getting the pain out and sharing it."
—Dennis Hopper

"JIMMY AND I COULD HAVE RUN HOLLYWOOD!"

Dennis Hopper

Like his old friend James Dean, Dennis Hopper has been a one-of-a-kind in Hollywood, a true rebel, seemingly without a cause. His career as an actor and director has had more ups and downs than a cardiogram. Over the past couple of years, however, he appears to have gotten his life and career back on track, with celebrated roles in such films as Blue Velvet and as the director of the controversial and successful Colors.

Along the way, his name made it into film history with Easy Rider, the 1969 film he wrote, directed and starred in. He also costarred as a war-dazed photographer in Francis Coppola's Apocalypse Now. But to James Dean fans, Dennis Hopper is first and foremost the handsome young man who appeared with Dean in Rebel Without a Cause and Giant.

Hopper spoke with SH-BOOM about his special friendship with the legendary actor he calls his mentor.

When I was 18 or 19, I thought I was the best actor around, or going to be. Then I met James Dean. Every time I smoke a cigarette short, I think of Jimmy. Jimmy said to me, 'Just smoke the cigarette, or drink the coffee. Don't think about it, just do it. React.' Jimmy gave me lots of advice and tips. So I started doing things. Like, I'd smoke a certain way, open a door differently....Like, you're alone in a room. There's the reality of the cameras, and you have to just accept it and feel you're alone in the room, regardless of the surroundings. Use simple reality. [You look at] just a person or an object. Then you reproduce a gesture, an attitude, a moment-to-moment reality.

"Imagination helps to reinforce you. Jimmy's mother died, and he'd go and cry at her grave. 'Why did you leave me?' He said, 'I'm gonna show you. I'm going to be something.' *That* we had in common; my dad died when I was young. Relax as an actor and feel the tension points. Jimmy taught me that. Use all your senses. Use and draw on only one sense in order to speak and recall a certain feeling or mood [from your past] for a reaction. Wear your emotional background.

"You know, if Jimmy Dean had lived, I think he and I could have run Hollywood!"—*Cherry Rees.*

SH-BOOM 27

A recent article in SH-BOOM magazine, June 1990

author collection

"I know by heart all the dialogue of James Dean's films. I could watch REBEL a hundred times over."
—Elvis Presley

"Dean had an astonishing hold on adolescent imagination; he brought authority to the role of the 'crazy-mixed-up kid'."
—Joe Morella, THE REBEL HERO IN FILMS

"...I found him to be an intelligent young actor who seemed to live only for his work. He was completely dedicated and although a shy person he could hold a good conversation on many wide-ranging subjects."
— Ronald Reagan

"Jimmy was absolutely suicidal with a car. People just stayed away because they didn't want to get killed. I'm not saying that he wasn't gifted as a race-car driver, but that extra irresponsible attitude towards his own life, I think, influenced his winning very often."
— Leonard Rosenman

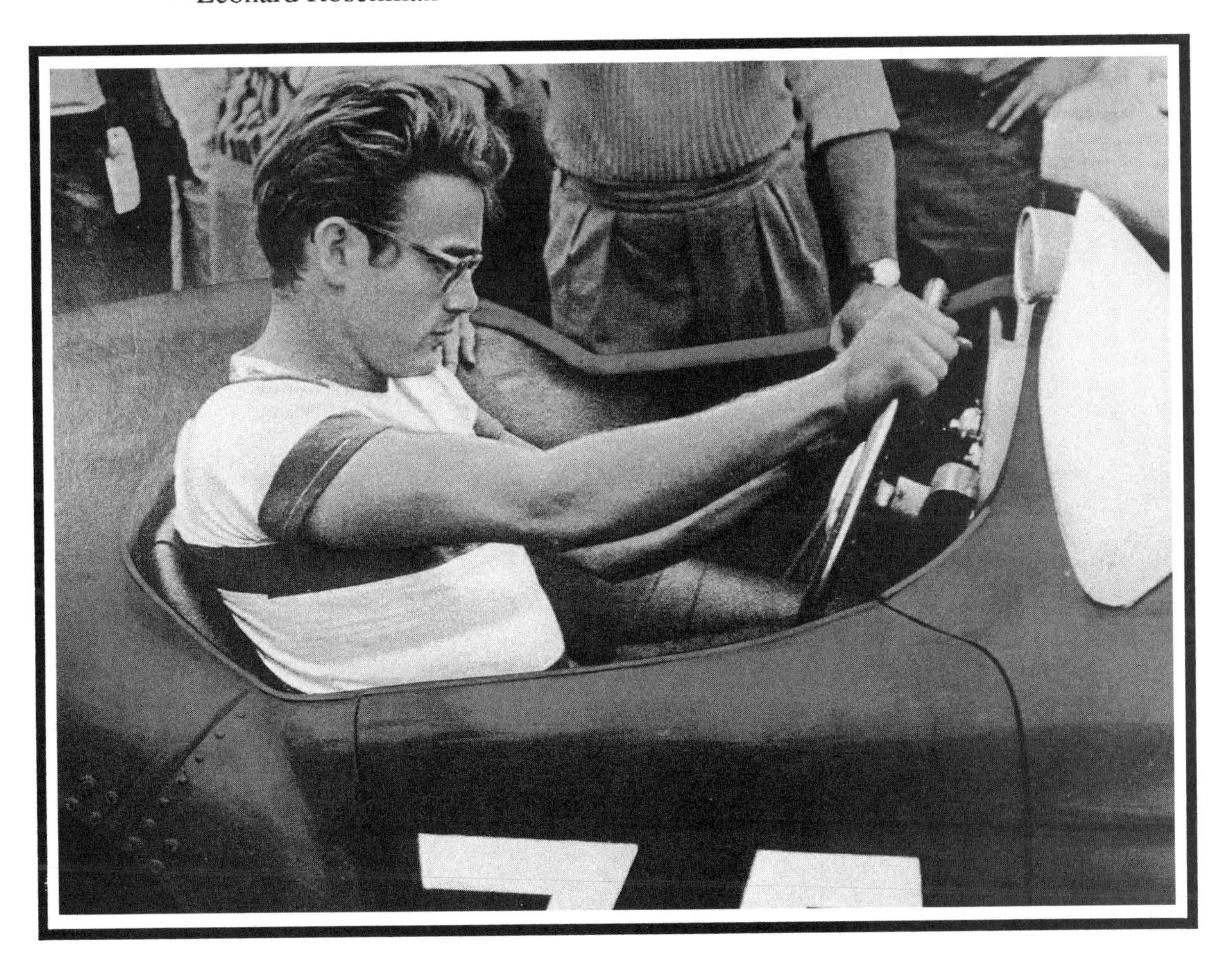

Warner Brothers
THE JAMES DEAN STORY

author collection

DEANMANIA

"In James Dean, today's youth discovers itself. Less for the reasons usually advanced—violence, sadism, hysteria, pessimism, cruelty and filth— than for others infinitely more simple and commonplace: modesty of feeling, continual fantasy life, moral purity without relation to everyday morality but all the more rigorous eternal adolescent love of tests and trails, intoxication, pride and regret at feeling 'outside' society, refusal and desire to become integrated and, finally, acceptance—or refusal—of the world as it is."
— Francois Truffaut, ARTS, September 1956

"I think had he lived he would probably have surpassed anybody that we have in the motion picture industry today."
—Paul Newman

"Dean represented the defeated teenager: sensitive, incoherent, rebellious, moody, grave, the victim of adult misunderstanding. What's more, his early death secured him instant and comparatively permanent beatification. I went to see one of his films the other day and a large section of the audience were young enough to have been children when it was first released. Yet the atmosphere was reverent, almost church-like. Death is the one certain way to preserve a pop legend, because age, itself is considered a compromise."
— George Melly, REVOLT IN SYTLE

"He was desperately lonely and had many inward problems, so it was hard to get close to him. He was a strange and sensitive character with tremendous imagination."
— Julie Harris

Warner Brothers EAST OF EDEN

author collection

"The night he was killed I was having dinner with a lot of his friends—Sal Mineo, Dick Davalos, Nick Adams. We were talking about Jimmy's lifestyle and Nick ventured the opinion that Jimmy wouldn't live till thirty. We pooh-poohed the idea. Later, when we finished eating, Nick and Sal walked me to my hotel. I was still underage then with a studio chaperone, and it was she who heard the news. She told Nick and Sal and asked them not to say anything to me because I had an early call the next day and she wanted me to sleep. So they left rather abruptly. Next morning the chaperone had to tell me because down in the lobby the newspapers had it on all the headlines. I didn't believe it. I think I stood at the window staring out for a long time. I went to work in a state of shock."
—Natalie Wood

Warner Brothers REBEL WITHOUT A CAUSE Natalie Wood and Sal Mineo
author collection

"Jimmy Dean started the entire youth movement. And a lot of young people today, in looking back, realize—even though they weren't even born when he died—that he was the first rebel: he was the first guy to ask all the questions: 'Why? Why?' He was the first one to give teenagers an identification of any kind. Before Jimmy Dean you were a baby or you were a man. In between was just one of those terrible stages that you had to get out of rather quickly. And he didn't. He gave the teenager a status."
—Sal Mineo

"There was no chance of knowing Jimmy any better than Jimmy wanted you to..."
— Mercedes McCambridge

"I introduced Jimmy to Humphrey Bogart, thinking they would hit it off. Bogie did most of the talking while Jimmy sat, literally, at his feet. It was a surprise to me that he was as star-struck as any tourist. I liked him all the more for it."
— Joe Hyams

"I joined the cast of GIANT after a long absence from the movies. I wasn't sure I could catch up. I met Jimmy. He was the most wonderful tease in the world. He made me laugh, guessing that's what I needed."
— Jane Withers

"Jimmy secretly wanted to be a baggy pants comedian and was quietly working on a nightclub act. Believe me, he would have 'killed the people'"
— Jim Backus

Warner Brothers REBEL WITHOUT A CAUSE James Dean, Ann Doran, Jim Backus/

author collection

"I felt that he was a disturbed boy, tremendously dedicated to some intangible beacon of his own, and neither he nor anyone else would know what it was.
"He had it coming to him. The way he drove he had it coming to him."
— George Stevens

Warner Brothers GIANT George Stevens director with James Dean on set at Marfa Texas

author collection

"Directing James Dean was like directing Lassie. I either lectured him or terrorized him, flattered him furiously or kicked his backside. He was so instinctive and so stupid in so many ways."
— Elia Kazan

"I didn't pick Jimmy for Rebel, we sniffed each other out, like a couple of Siamese cats. We went to New York together so I could see where he lived. You should have seen his room—a tiny place, cluttered with books and boxes."
— Nick Ray

"He's not an idol of mine, and I didn't particularly like what he was."
— Elia Kazan

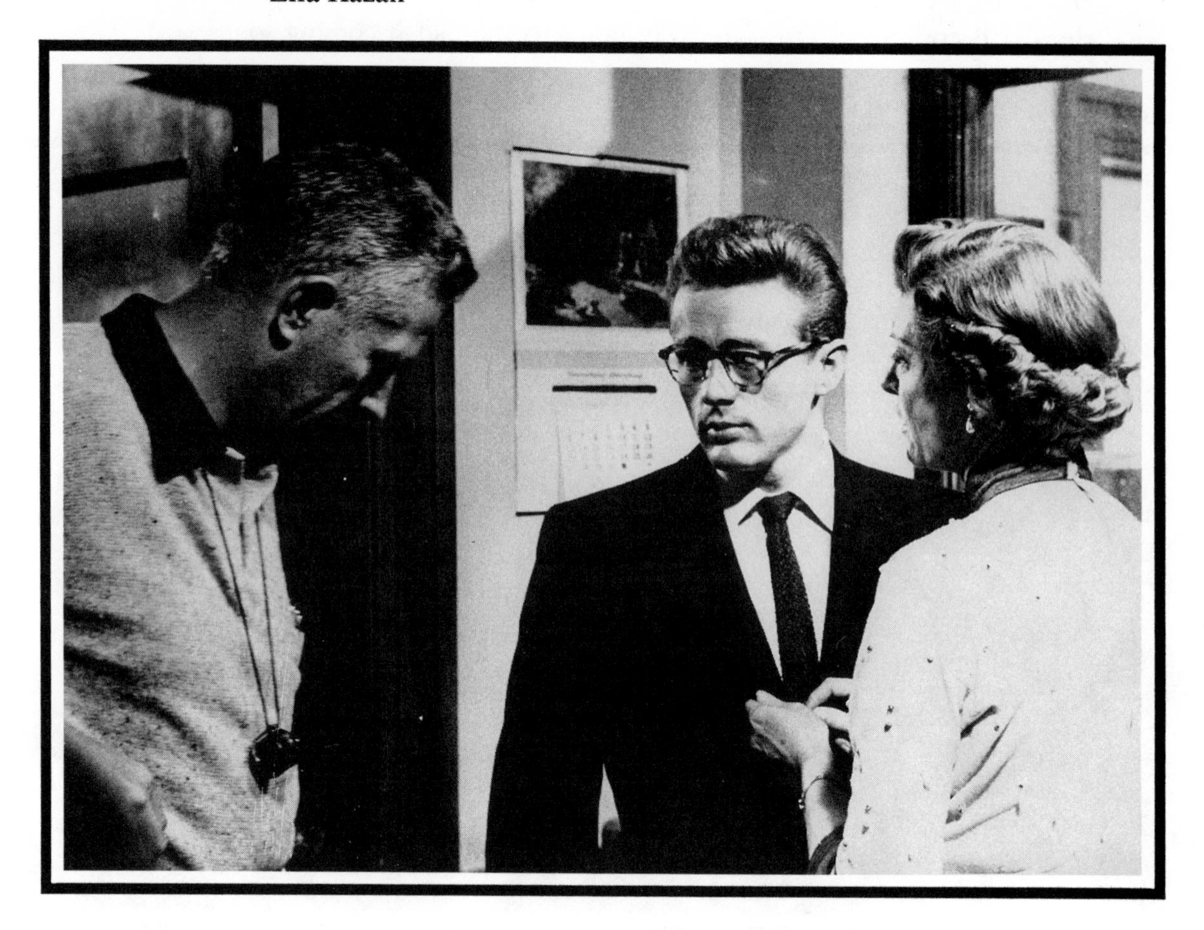

Warner Brothers REBEL WITHOUT A CAUSE Director Nick Ray with James Dean and Ann Doran author collection

"I realized that I was dealing with a talent that was pure gold. I said to him, 'Jimmy people will be watching that long after we've gone and they'll still think it's great.' This seemed to please him tremendously."
— Elia Kazan

"In every respect he was the Cal of Steinbeck's novel. He was to become a sort of cult with the young. Jimmy had only to act himself. But that is a difficult role even for an experienced actor to play. A rebel at heart, he approached everything with a chip on his shoulder...You know and we all know that Jimmy's got it. He's good. But there are rules to go by in our profession and he'd better abide by them. One is to stick to the script."
— Raymond Massey

"One felt that he was a boy one had to take care of, but even that was probably his joke. I don't think he needed anybody or anything—except his acting."
— Elizabeth Taylor

"The whole time I worked with the man I never got a civil word out of him. He always seemed resentful about something."
— Rock Hudson

"Anyone who came into contact with Jimmy found that their lives were never quite the same again. God knows where a spirit like that comes from. They flash across our lives like a shooting star."
— Elizabeth Taylor

"There's alot of jealousy about Jimmy in terms of 'Why should he have all this adoration? Why should people still have a kind of thing about him?' Well, there are only two people in the world that I can remember, within my lifetime, that created that. One was Marilyn Monroe, and the other was James Dean. It's very funny—if you get four or five people around who knew Jim, everyone has a story to tell that they remember. Everyone has something to say about it. But if you put'em all together, it almost sounds as if you're telling about four or five different people."
— Sammy Davis Jr.

"I think Dean died at the right time. Had he lived he would never have been able to keep up with all that publicity."
— Humphrey Bogart

Warner Brothers THE JAMES DEAN STORY

author collection

Fans, young and old, remember James Dean...

REBEL STAR

Oh, rebel star glowing bright
Like a comet in the night
Other stars have come and gone
Still your brightness lingers on.

Many mortals saw your birth
Soaring high above the earth
There were a few who had doubt
Thinking you would soon burn out.

Thirty years have passed us by
You still illuminate the sky
No other star can lay this claim
That after death there still is fame.

Circling ever round this sphere
New generations still revere
The light their elders breathless saw
And now they, too, stare in awe.

Oh! Rebel star ever bright
Still adding brilliance to the night
Still the brightest to be seen
And the name they gave you — DEAN.
—Philip Zeigler (9/15/84),
"We Remember Dean Newsletter"

"It is not because of his status of American icon or rebel that I admire James Dean, although I would be lying if I didn't say that the aspect appealed to me at first. Just what Jimmy means to me I can't seem to capture in limited, heartless words. I guess you could sum it all up like this, James Dean is a special feeling that every fan holds deep down inside their hearts."
—Randy Cox, Canada

"James Dean may be the mirror of my dream,
Or a clear reflection in a stream,
But the shadows of his past,
I'll remember until the day I die,
And his laughter and his tears,
I'll make my souvenirs."
— Sarah King, England

"James Dean's life was over long before I came into existence, yet I'm attracted to the actor, the person, the legend. I first saw his face on a poster two years ago. I immediately bought it. And that, as the cliche goes, is how it all started. I knew the first time I saw his countenance that I had to know all I could about him. I learned that the face had a life and a personality. I learned that this pained young man had a story to tell the world, that many were willing to listen. This man was more than a curiosity, he was an obsession to thousands."
— Catherine Andrews, Virginia

"I'm nineteen...I have been a fan of James Dean for several years now, and I am still captivated each time I see one of his three films. What an amazing gift he possessed! There has never been another actor who so deeply touched my heart and soul..."
— Tammi Shaw, Wisconsin

"Jimmy knew what young people were up against!"
— an admirer

"I, too, am a James Dean devoted fan. I became this after viewing EAST OF EDEN. I cried three times during my viewing of it! It really touched me. It wasn't just the great story by John Steinbeck, but it was Dean's portrayal of Cal Trask. It was because of Dean that the movie was a success and considered, by many, one of the world's best movies..."
— Samara A. Rosa, Wisconsin

"I have been an admirer of Jimmy since I first saw EAST OF EDEN when I was seventeen. (I'm now 24). I can't really describe the feeling I had when I first saw that picture, other than to say I'd never seen anyone like him before (and I'm sure I will never see anyone like him again). I started watching the films and reading

books on him. Asking my mom what she recalled of him, she vividly remembered going to see REBEL three or four times when she was a teenager and said she was not surprised at his popularity today."
— Darryl Rabideau, New York

"I am 17 years old and a huge James Dean fan. I discovered him when I was 15. Ever since then, I have been fascinated with the short but meaningful life of this wonderful actor. I see parts of myself in his emotions and feelings as a teen."
— Terri Caton

"I'm fascinated with James Dean and I attribute most of that fascination to the fact that I can't really explain why. I've also been interested in movie personalities, but not until I watched Jimmy on the screen for the first time in GIANT did I see that his abilities as an actor will never be surpassed by any other. I quickly got my hands on EDEN and REBEL and was completely transfixed for the entire duration of both movies. I believe everyone in the world could identify with some aspect of Jimmy's personality. The roles in which he acted were three totally different people, yet he enveloped each one completely."
— Christy Martin

Two portraits of James Dean painted by fans Ed Lane (above) and M. Baker (below) and donated to the Fairmount Historical Museum

courtesy of the Fairmount Historical Museum

"...I am 20 years old. Ever since I saw EAST OF EDEN on Dutch television about five years ago I have been a big fan of Jimmy Dean. Before that I had never heard of him. So, as I was deeply impressed by him, and the way he acted, I wanted to know more about him."
— Patricia Troost, Netherlands

"I am a James Dean fan after seeing his movies on South African television. James represents for me a lonely person who longs to have friends and longs to be loved. I became a fan in 1989, after seeing a clipping in the local newspaper. James is the person who everyone can relate to in their emotions."
— Shelley Rootenberg , Cape Province, Republic of South Africa

"I am only 14 but I love James Dean. His acting is superb. There is something about him that got me interested in him so I rented all of his movies and I loved them! I really want to know more about him..."
— Sara Montgomery, North Carolina

"I am 17 years old and I have been an admirer of James Dean for two years. I am not sure exactly what or why I started liking him. I hadn't seen any of his movies nor had I seen any pictures of him, but I did read a short article about

him in the local newspaper on the anniversary of his death.

That got me thinking, so I asked my parents about him and they told me about the things they felt when they heard of his death. They were both 15 in 1955, and how he had touched so many people in his short time as a Hollywood movie star. So my initial intention in finding out about James Dean was to just see who he was and find out why so many people thought he was so special. Little did I know that you can't read and learn about James Dean without falling in love with him, or at least the memory of him. Since I have read all I can and seen all three of his movies, even bought two of them, and also posters, books, and so on..."

— Megan Rush, Arizona

James Dean portrait painted by F. Hollis (above) and donated to the Fairmount Historical Museum.
courtesy Fairmount Historical Museum

"My name is Mary Jo and although I'm only 19 and too young to have been around in the 1950s, I am a fan of James Dean. I guess what I like about Jimmy is that he is forever young. His acting was something he deeply got into (unlike many actors and actresses of today), and even though this might seem odd, his smile and mostly his laugh can brighten my worst day. I recently visited Fairmount on my way home from vacation and only had time to stop at The James Dean Gallery and I enjoyed everything. Being young I guess I identify with his 'Rebel' label. I'm not the rebellious type but where I go to college I get teased about my different points of view and my way of doing things. Once in a while someone will say I'm a rebel (I don't think so!). Jimmy's wanting to be known, listened to, and understood is what I feel from his movies and I relate to that. I hope future generations can admire him and help keep him alive."

— Mary Jo Wilkinson, Michigan

Original ink sketch done by Norman Patterson in 1956
courtesy of Norman Patterson

"I am a Dean fan because he was the largest influence on my life. I relate to his 'not conforming' to society. His way of doing things better than anybody else. James Dean was one of a kind. He did not accept just anybody or anything pushed in front of him. No false standards for him. I became a 'Dean' fan in 1956. His outlook on life and massive talent impressed me. 'James Dean' fans from the 50s were hooked when is movies first came out. I think today's fans are following a trend caused by massive marketing of memorabilia."

— Norman Patterson, Republic of South Africa

"It's hard for me to explain why I'm a James Dean fan. Obviously his phenomenal acting had a great impact on me, but James Dean, the person, affected me just as strongly. His determination in life to be the best in everything he did has been an inspiration to me. I relate to him in many ways: his moodiness and loneliness; his hesitation to trust others; his sense of humor—even his nearsightedness...I appreciate the fact that he believed in himself and thought he could accomplish whatever he set out to do and he never let anything stop him! He knew he had to be an actor and he

strived to be the best!..His influence has been all-pervasive to subsequent generations, as well as his own. Teenagers love him and consider him, 'a real cool dude'. He'll always have that impact because he looked into the hearts and minds of all of us (rebels at any age) and he was able to portray what we FELT like. No one else was ever able to...."
— Marilyn Wells, California

Marilyn Wells carries an interest in James Dean to the extent that her license plate bears how she feels about James Dean

courtesy of Marilyn Wells

"I am a James Dean fan because I have found so many reasons to respect this person. I respect him for having so much courage and strength to survive in a world that he didn't seem to understand. He dedicated so much of his heart, soul, and spirit into doing what he loved to do (acting). He didn't seem to let all of the outside forces of society break him. He remained an individual throughout his twenty-four years. He shows me that you do not have to be extremely experienced or trained, or out-going to succeed in 'the business.' He inspires me greatly. He helps me to make me believe in myself. He helps to give my spirit a push in the right direction when I can't seem to do it myself."
— Gayle Grove, West Virginia

"I am a fan because he seemed to always be looking for something that was missing in his life, and I believe we all have this in common with one another. He represents a kind of freedom..."
— Michael Bundy, Indiana

"...He shows so many emotions, usually at the same time, anger, sadness, bitterness...Jimmy represents eternal youth...Dean means...a little of everything—youth, sensitivity, warmth, caring...Jimmy had it all—charm, looks, personality...I can't think of any young actor today who has the charisma to last as long as Jimmy. So you tell me—was he ever real or just a figment of my imagination?"
— Tammy Epperson, Ohio

"I am a James Dean fan for many reasons. First of all, I feel that his interpretations of the characters he portrayed—from St. John the Apostle in the 1951 TV drama 'Hill Number One'—to his final characterization, 'Jett Rink', were probably among the most brillant, exciting, and unforgettable ever put on film. Secondly, I considered him a kind of American 'Renaissance Man' who seemed to be able to do ANYTHING—from basketball to acting, from auto-racing to sculpting—and do it so well. Thirdly, he was easily the most photogenic individual I've ever seen. That alone makes him aesthetically special...I feel that his ultimate goal was to leave behind a legacy that would be impossible to ignore; not as an ego-stroke, but as a gift to posterity as well as to the future generations of young people whom he must have believed would continue to see themselves in him—AND vice-versa...I believe that Jimmy's fans, who remember when he was alive, will remember him basically because of the sheer power of his personality. He possessed that magical quality—CHARISMA—before most people even knew what the word meant. (I am not sure that we yet know what it means). I think he had more style and class than anyone that young, in my lifetime, at least. I also think he single-handedly set the standard for what millions of teenagers-to-come would define as 'COOL'. To me, it's an attitude—being bound and determined to do it 'your way'. I think it's safe to assume that it's the attitude that makes him attractive to this generation of young people. Personally, I will always remember James Dean for his tremendous desire for knowledge—his constant struggle for growth and improvement as a person—and his commitment to living life to its fullest."
— Tom Pevarnik, Pennsylvania

RIGHT: A portrait painted by Jill Downen and donated to the Fairmount Historical Museum

courtesy of the Fairmount Historical Museum

LEFT: A fan from France painted and donated two portraits of James Dean to the Fairmount Historical Museum. This is one of two paintings displayed

courtesy of the Fairmount Historical Museum

James Dean - Memoria et Aeterna

September 30, 1960

Text courtesy of Fairmount Histtorical Museum

Within these walls, JAMES DEAN, while still a student, took the first public steps of his magnificent ascent to the very summit of one of life's highest mountains. Within a brief time, he had found there, not only a place of immortality for himself, but new honors for his art, his country, and his native city, as well.

Though the years for accomplishment allotted him were few, his stirring story has been one of such beauty and magnitude that there remains no man living today to whom, as any artist, so many of this world's millions feel and have acknowledged so great an indebtedness for the ennobling impulses which, even now, spring freely from him and his memory. A golden legend even in his time, he was one of the few young artists of true genius our age has produced. He was one whose amazingly sensitive art bespoke such truth and beauty that it has transcended all barriers of race and tongue and reached people of all ages in many different lands. In fact, he spoke the universal language which comes only from the mysterious gift of artistic genius. Like the birds which sing, this can never be stilled. The many, everywhere, have not missed his meaning and only the blessed few can ever possess such a spark. It is genius's open secret to be able, as if with a magic rod, to generate a power so deeply soulful that it penetrates to the innermost depths of man's being. So it was, that when he spoke there was much more to hear than mere words—so strong was the impact of his presence that we continue to be moved by something far more than just thought. In reaching to the deepest human levels, he was able to lift the eyes of many everywhere, to sights far removed from anything looked upon before and away from themselves. In leaving this supreme legacy, JAMES DEAN not only far exceeded any dream which might have been his, but from his lofty height established a new and many-splendoured rainbow providing a never ending source of human inspiration. It will remain shining in the skies as long as people will remember and can look heavenward.

There have been, of course, other great artists, magnificently gifted and a blessing to the world. There has never been one who has, in the tenderest years of adulthood, so genuinely moved human hearts around the globe, as has he. When he would gaze far away, over the heads of his audience, as though into some private heaven, there would immediately arise an understanding and communication so deep that it consciously flashed from face to face with an electric spark, radiant and thrilling, and exploding in thunderous world plaudits which sprang from deeply moved hearts. It must be said that his "audience could not cough or look aside without loss." Therefore, let all who know, in truth, the greatness which began its simple evolution here, regard it well and know it better. Those who have known and seen him with admiration, and certainly those yet to see and know, will never cease to join the chorus which sings the enduring words of Royden:

> **"Was never eye did see that face,**
> **Was never ear did hear that tongue,**
> **Was never mind did mind his grace,**
> **That ever thought the travail long,**
> **But eyes and ears and every thought,**
> **Were with his sweet perfections caught."**

Two rows of photos which tell Dean's life from young child through the filming of GIANT

Courtesy Fairmount Historical Museum

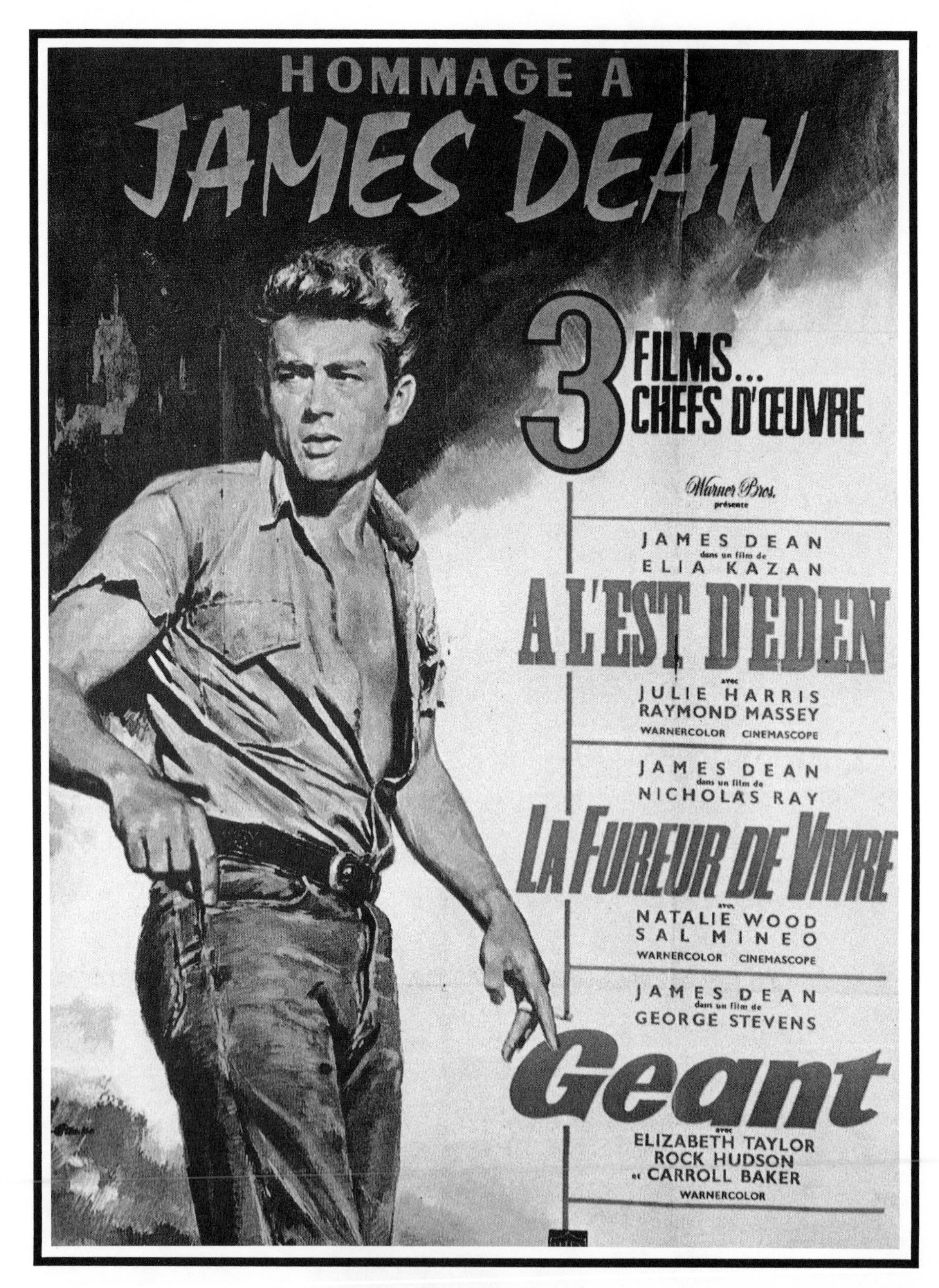

French salute to
James Dean and his three films.

PART TWO

James Dean: The Character

"An actor must interpret life and in order to do so he must be willing to accept all experiences that life has to offer. In fact, he must seek out more of life than life puts at his feet. In the short span of his lifetime an actor must learn all there is to know, experience all there is to experience, or approach that state as closely as possible. He must be superhuman in his efforts to store away in the warehouse of his subconscious everything that he might be called upon to use in the expression of his art. Nothing should be more important to the artist than life and the living of it, not even the ego. To grasp the ful significance of life is the actor's duty; to interpret it his problem; and to express it his dedication...
Being an actor is the loneliest thing in the world. You're all alone with your concentration and imagination, and that's all you have. Being a good actor isn't easy. Being a man is even harder. I want to be both before I'm done."

— James Dean

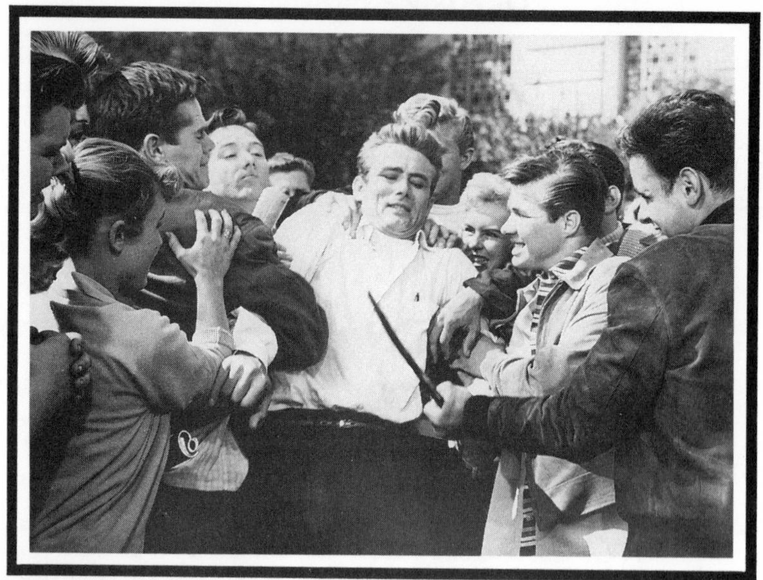

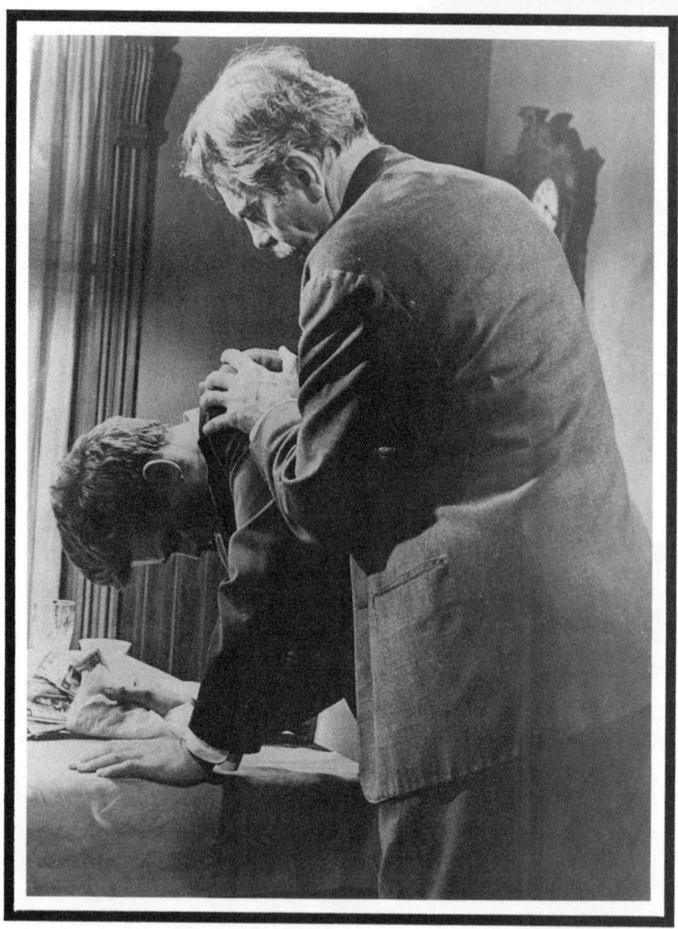

The three faces of James Dean, The Character.
TOP LEFT: As Jim the Rebel Without a Cause
LEFT: As Cal in East of Eden
BOTTOM RIGHT: As Jett in Giant

Dean: The Character

"I think he was pure gold. That image he created on the screen, the three roles that he played are as contemporary today as they were when they were made. I think there's no question he was one of the greatest actors that ever lived."

— Dennis Hopper

The fact that James Dean's movie career lasted only a short sixteen months, and that within that brief period of time he was able to participate in three cinematic greats, demonstrates clearly the extent to which he was able to create on film, characters who remain for us today as contemporary as when he first stepped before the cameras and created them.

Few would argue that our understanding of James Dean, both as a person and as a legend, is due in large part to his characterizations of Cal Trask, Jim Stark, and Jett Rink. Dennis Stock recalls for us how Dean in his first role as Cal Trask, "expressed hues and shadowings of adolescence that had probably never been seen before. I and the movie audience clearly empathized with Cal as Dean led us masterfully through his plight of alienation and innocence. Capitalizing on the limits of the adolescent's ability to articulate, Dean used his body to the utmost. His expressions were exceptionally graphic. Literally on the edge of my seat throughout the screening, I mentally photographed his rich variety of powerful gestures."

If indeed Dean created such an impression on Stock, then it should hardly be surprising that such was not the case for countless other individuals who saw EAST OF EDEN. For many, including some who knew Dean well, the only opportunity they had to understand Dean was through the characters he portrayed in film.

While the film EAST OF EDEN gave Dean the exposure he desperately wanted, according to David Dalton there remains no question that this film also "was important to Jimmy, not only because it was his first starring role, but also because he identified so strongly with its heroic theme. In this role, Jimmy relied on his ability as a chameleon to slip from mask to mask, occasionally giving us an intimate glimpse of the vulnerable spirit who would flash a look" of the James Dean that his friends and colleagues wished so much to know.

In the role of Cal Trask, James Dean was able to draw from his experiences and his abilities as an actor. He would communicate much that he was unable to say in his own life.

It is in Dean's characterization of Jim Stark that we are able to further understand the "real" James Dean. Ronald Martinetti, as well as countless other writers, and those who knew Dean well, assert that REBEL WITHOUT A CAUSE is the quintessential Dean film. Martinetti writes that this film, "the one in which, the legend maintained, Dean was playing himself: the sensitive delinquent, the original crazy mixed-up kid who, as Pauline Kael put it 'does everything wrong because he cares so much.'"

Further, David Dalton in JAMES DEAN THE MUTANT KING leads us to understand that in REBEL WITHOUT A CAUSE Dean "dominates, absorbs, and incorporates its drama as both victim and hero, and he injects the film with all the diffuse fragments of his own personality. In his role, he reveals all that we know about Jimmy as James Dean." Again, James Dean has revealed to us something about himself.

Dean completes the trilogy with his portrayal of Jett Rink. Perhaps his most challenging role, yet the one he seems to have received the least acclaim for. In EAST OF EDEN we see Dean as the loner; in REBEL WITHOUT A CAUSE he is the rebel, and in GIANT he becomes the "anti-hero".

What seems most striking about about his role in the film GIANT is that according to Robert Benayoum, he is able to "convey a profound moral distress, a fundamental insecurity, which were, moreover, his own...Whether Jimmy Dean would have worn the face he composed here had he lived we shall never know. His old age remains imaginary, mythic, improbable..." The fact that James Dean does indeed age as Jett Rink would seem to be a plausible explanation as to why this movie is the least popular among the three films.

While Dean's characterization of Rink as an old man may indeed remain "imaginary, mythic, and improbable" given the circumstances as they exist, there is no question as to the effectiveness with which he was able to convey old age in his role as Jett Rink. John Howlett recalls that "Dean had so mastered the physical presence of an older man, that when he met Sal Mineo one day in the studios, Mineo did not recognize him..."

James Dean in his characterizations of Cal Trask, Jim Stark, and Jett Rink allows us to see who he was without his having to tell us. It is important however to remember that a person as complicated as James Dean can not be entirely understood through three character portrayals. Attention should be given to Dean's early television performances.

Fortunately many of the early television appearances are now available. These early TV appearances provide us with another dimension of James Dean The Character.

There is little doubt that each character, portrayed by James Dean on the screen and preserved for us today on film, pervades his life and person. The extent to which this occurs depends entirely upon the interpretation of his performance and how it fits into what we know about James Dean. James Dean The Character provides us with another dimension.

Leonard Rosenman, a friend of Dean's perhaps best sums it up:

"Jimmy had, in my estimation, a severe identity problem—he really didn't know who he was. He certainly identified with the roles that were given him, and I think that roles—these roles of Cal and the rebellious boy in REBEL WITHOUT A CAUSE and the rebellious ranch-hand in GIANT —were given to him because he was that to a degree. Except, there was a kind of an unfortunate evolution in the closet, because he had no real identity himself."

The Films of James Dean

Dean: The Films

For each of the films included, the following information is provided:

1) **RATINGS** given to each film by Leonard Maltin, TV MOVIES AND VIDEO GUIDE (1990); Steven Scheuer, MOVIES ON TV (1989); Martin and Porter, VIDEO MOVIE GUIDE (1990); and MOTION PICTURE GUIDE (1986).

2) **CREDITS** including cast members, crew and production staff;

3) **FILM SYNOPSIS** as provided by studio campaign materials;

4) **FILM FACTS** including premiere dates as well as interesting points of information about the film;

5) **FILM REVIEWS**; and

6) **ILLUSTRATIONS** including movie stills, movie posters and lobby cards, and videotape jackets. Each videotape jacket is included here and used only for illustration. They are the copyright of the respective videotape publisher.

Videotapes are available from the following publishers:

Warner Home Video, Warner Communications Co
4000 Warner Blvd., Burbank, CA 91522

VidAmerica, Inc., 235 E. 55th Street, New York, NY 10022

TAV Inc., 627 Montrose Ave., South Plainfield, NJ 07080

Pacific Arts Video Records, Pacific Arts Bldg., Carmel, CA 93923

Mary Ann Michna, 1440 W. Jefferson, #3W, Des Plaines, IL 60016

While Dean's three movies, the three documentaries, and THE JAMES DEAN STORY are readily found in most video stores or from the publishers noted above, his television appearances are more difficult to obtain. Included in this film guide is as complete a list of television appearances as has been compiled. The majority of Dean's early work in television remains largely in the hands of a few collectors who have been able to secure copies over the last few years.

All photography appearing in this section is the property of the respective copyright holders. The identity of these copyright holders is often difficult to ascertain with certainty, and each appears only for illustrative purposes. Most have been selected from the author's collection or collections of other fans. In no way is any intent to infringe on the rights of the copyright holders intended by the author, publisher or any other party.

Hopefully, this James Dean film guide will provide an opportunity to explore his movies and the roles he created on film in greater detail, thereby enabling each of us to reach a greater appreciaton for JAMES DEAN THE CHARACTER.

JAMES DEAN

IN THE ROLE
THAT ZOOMED HIM
TO STARDOM!

ELIA KAZAN'S PRODUCTION OF JOHN STEINBECK'S

"EAST OF EDEN"

The most
shocking
revenge
a girl
ever let
one brother
take on
another!

This is
James Dean
hailed as "the most
dynamic star discovery
of the year" by LOOK magazine!

WARNER BROS. PRESENT IT IN AN INTIMATE NEW USE OF CINEMASCOPE AND WARNERCOLOR

STARRING

JULIE HARRIS · JAMES DEAN · RAYMOND MASSEY

with

BURL IVES · RICHARD DAVALOS · JO VAN FLEET · LOIS SMITH

Screen Play by Directed by

Ratings

Maltin: ****

Scheuer: ****

Martin/Porter: *****

Motion Picture Guide: *****

East of Eden

Warner Bros., 1955

CREDITS

CAST
Cal Trask (James Dean); Abra (Julie Harris); Adam Trask (Raymond Massey); Aaron Trask (Richard Davalos); Sam Cooper, Sheriff (Burl Ives); Kate (Jo Van Fleet); Will Hamilton (Albert Dekker); Anne (Lois Smith); Mr. Albrecht (Harold Gordon); Dr. Edwards (Richard Garrick); Joe (Timothy Carey); Rantani (Nick Dennis); Roy (Lonnie Chapman); Nurse (Barbara Baxley); Barmaid (Bette Treadville); Bartender (Tex Mooney); Bouncer (Harry Cording); Card Dealer (Loretta Rush); Coalman (Bill Phillips); Piscora (Mario Siletti); Piscora's son (Jonathan Haze); Carnival People (Jack Carr, Roger Creed, Effie Laird, Wheaton Chambers, Ed Clark, Al Ferguson, Franklyn Farnum, Rose Plummer); Photographer (John George); English Officer (C. Ramsey Hill); Soldier (Edward McNally); Shooting Gallery Attendant (Earle Hodgins)

CREW
Directed by Elia Kazan
Screenplay by Paul Osborn, based upon the novel by John Steinbeck
Music by Leonard Roseman
Director of Photography: Ted McCord
Art Dir: James Basevi, Malcolm Bert
Edited by Owen Marks

Film Facts :

Premiere:

April 10, 1955.
The only film of Dean to be released while he was still living.

* A special celebrity preview of EAST OF EDEN was held March 9, 1955 at Astor Theater on Broadway. This premiere was a benefit for the Actors Studio. Although many celebrities attended, one who absented himself was the star, James Dean. To his agent, Jane Deacy, he remarked, "I can't make this scene...I can't handle it."

Awards:

* James Dean was nominated for an Academy Award for his performance in this film. The Foreign Press honored the picture with the Golden Globe as Best Motion Picture/Drama. Jo Van Fleet won an Oscar for Best Supporting Actress.

Other Film Facts

* This was James Dean's screen debut.

* Filming began on May 27, 1954 and was completed on August 13, 1954.

* By March 1955 EAST OF EDEN had broken into VARIETY's list of top-grossing films and it wasn't long before it was number one. The movie set new box-office records across the country.

* Kazan's original cast included Marlon Brando as Cal and Montgomery Clift as Aaron.

* The cast included persons selected from the Actor's Studio, and the Motion Picture Academy's Casting Directory. There was not a box-office name in the entire cast.

* Dean received $20,000 for the film along with $4,000 as an advance.

* This movie served to project Dean as the symbol of America's disillusioned and disassociated youth.

* Because of the immediate star-status Dean acquired, Warner Brothers issued him a new contract, paying him $100,000 a movie. The first movie scheduled was REBEL WITHOUT A CAUSE.

* EAST OF EDEN's director Elia Kazan observed "[at] the end of shooting, the last few days, you felt a star was going to be born. Everybody smelled it; all the publicity people began to hang around him."

* Most critics and friends alike believe that EAST OF EDEN allowed James Dean to communicate to many what he could not say in real life.

THE STORY....

Circa 1917. Among the students rushing from classes at the end of the day, Aaron Trask, the well-adjusted and upstanding son, and his girl friend, Abra, are joined by Aaron's brother, Cal, the troubled and troublesome son, who believes that his brother is loved and he is not. He then follows the couple to an ice house where their father, Adam Trask, a Bible-reading lettuce farmer, is excitedly explaining to Will Hamilton his plan to keep vegetables fresh by refrigeration. In introducing his two sons, Adam plainly reveals that Aaron is his favorite.

That evening, Cal learns from sheriff Sam Cooper that his mother, who deserted Adam years before, is Kate, owner of a notorious gambling and dance hall. When Adam's refrigeration project fails, Cal, anxious to win his father's affection, enters into a profitable venture with Will.

One night at an amusement park, Cal offers Abra a ride on the ferris wheel. She protests her love for Aaron but passionately returns Cal's kisses.

At Adam's birthday celebration, Cal makes elaborate preparations to present to his father all the profits from the speculation. When Cal approaches Adam and proceeds to offer him the money from his enterprise to supplant his losses, Adam rejects the money, learning how Cal made it and considering it tainted.

Adam then reprimands his son for profiteering and Cal is further denounced by his brother. With that, Cal decides to reveal the secret of their mother.

Following the meeting with his mother and discovering Abra's love for Cal, it is an Aaron, traumatized by the truth, who bides Adam farewell before departing to join the Army. Stricken by the turn of events, Adam is carried home. There, as Abra pleads, Adam finally acknowledges Cal, and blesses them both.

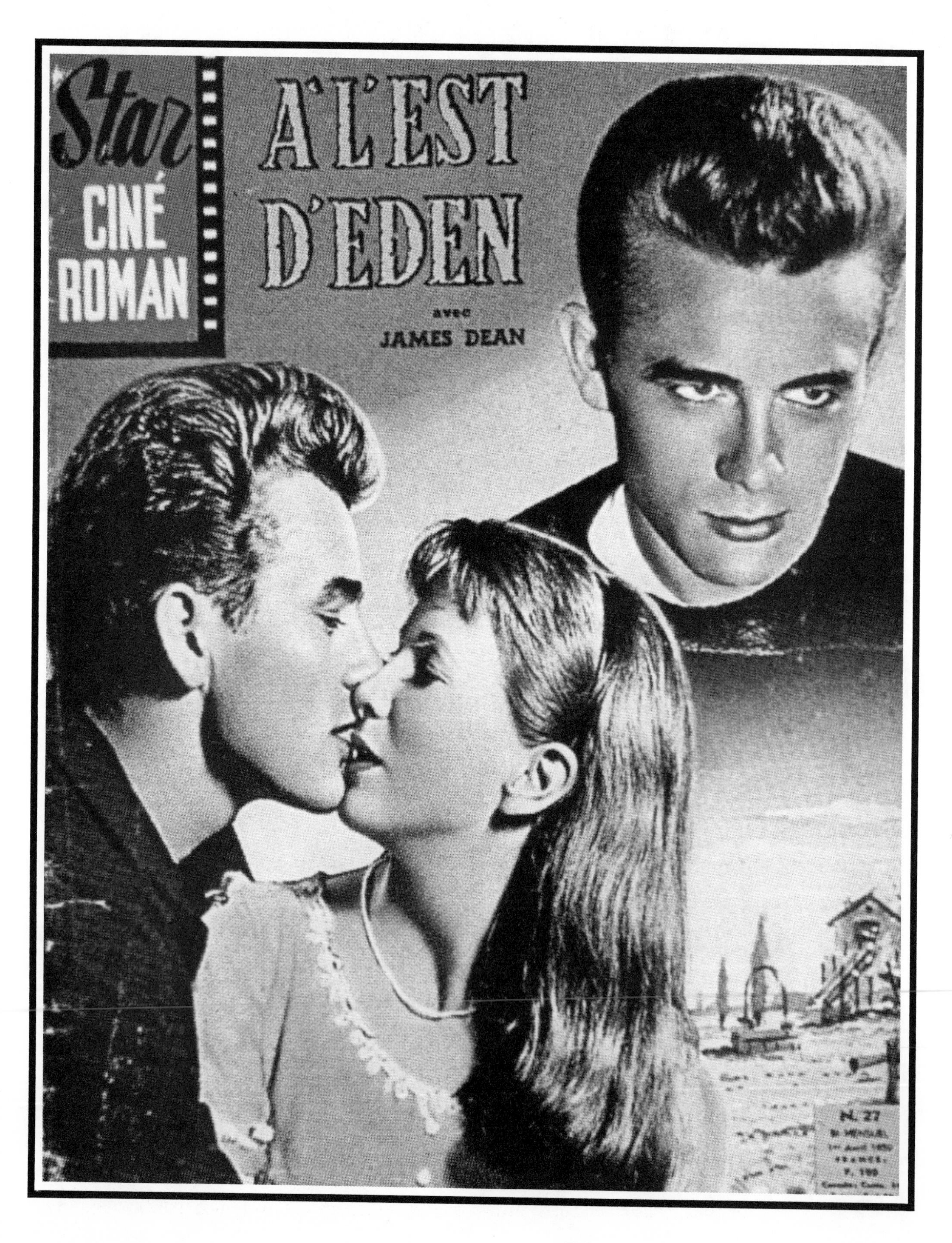

Star
CINÉ
ROMAN
A L'EST
D'EDEN
avec
JAMES DEAN
N. 27

East of Eden: The Critics

THE DAILY NEWS: "When the last scene faded from the Astor Theatre screen last night a new star appeared...James Dean." -Kate Cameron

CHICAGO TRIBUNE: Writes that Dean gave "the best performance of the year." -Herb Lyon

NEW YORK TIMES (February 27, 1955): "March 10th—Astor, B'way at 45th St. ELIA KAZAN—JOHN STEINBECK—AND THE 'SOMETHING' THAT MEANS 'EVERYTHING' IN MOTION PICTURE GREATNESS! Ask anybody—EAST OF EDEN is Steinbeck's masterpiece. Its sons and lovers, its saints and sinners, its losers and winners all have the look of, and the yen for, life. If these bone-saw, flesh-real people stormed almost bodily off Steinbeck's electric pages, you can imagine what happens to them in the hands of Elia Kazan, who just about invented screen realism as it is known today. EAST OF EDEN is one for the book—the one where they keep all the records of all the awards!...This is James Dean—a very special new star!"

TIME (March 21, 1955): "The picture is brilliant entertainment and more than that, it announces a new star, James Dean, whose prospects look as bright as any young actor's since Marlon Brando...Dean, a young man from Indiana, is unquestionably the biggest news Hollywood has made in 1955...Dean tries so hard to find the part in himself that he often forgets to put himself into the part. But no matter what he is doing, he has the presence of a young lion and the same sense of danger about him. His eye is as empty as an animal's, and he lolls and gallops with the innocence and grace of an animal. Then, occasionally, he flicks a sly little look that seems to say: 'Well, all this is human, too—or had you forgotten?'"

THE HOLLYWOOD REPORTER: "QUALITY FILM BASED ON THE STEINBECK NOVEL. EXCELLENT PRODUCTION, ACTING AND DIRECTION. INTRODUCING JAMES DEAN WHO MAY BE A HYPO AT THE BOX OFFICE."

HEDDA HOPPER'S HOLLYWOOD (March 27, 1955). "JAMES DEAN: I can't remember when any screen newcomer generated as much excitement in Hollywood as did James Dean in his first picture, EAST OF EDEN "

MARION CHRONICLE-TIMES (April 6, 1955): "EAST OF EDEN STAR PRAISED BY TEACHER. 'It was beyond all we had expected,' Mrs. Adeline Nall, Fairmount High School speech teacher, said Tuesday of the performance by her former student, James Dean, in Warner Brothers' EAST OF EDEN ....'It didn't seem strange at all to watch Jim work in this fine movie,' Mrs. Nall said. 'All of us felt we were right there with him. Many of the movements of 'Cal Trask' were characteristic movements of James Dean,' she continued. 'His funny little laugh, which ripples with the slightest provocation; his quick, jerky, springy walks and actions; his sudden change from frivolity to gloom—all were just like Jim used to do...'"

German advertisement. Note significant difference in portrayal of characters.

Finish movie poster.

NEW YORK HERALD TRIBUNE: "He (Jimmy) will inevitably be compared to Marlon Brando, for Kazan has stamped him with the same hesitant manner of speech, the same blind groping for love and security that he gave Brando in ON THE WATERFRONT. But if the performances are akin, so are the roles, and to complain about the similarity would be quibbling...Everything about Dean suggests the lonely, misunderstood nineteen-year old. Even from a distance you know a lot about him by the way he walks—with his hands in his pockets and his head down, slinking like a dog waiting for a bone. When he talks, he stammers and pauses, uncertain of what he is trying to say. When he listens, he is full of restless energy—he stretches, he rolls on the ground, he chins himself on the porch railing, like a small boy impatient of his elders' chatter...Occasionally, he smiles unaccountably as if at some dark joke known only to him..." —William Zinsser

Later on March 13, 1955, William Zinsser follows his previous review with the following:
NEW YORK HERALD TRIBUNE: "In every mannerism, as well as in the things he says, Dean shapes this secretive character, rather like Hamlet in many ways, and we finally feel that we know him at least as well as his father does."

NEW YORK TIMES: "Only a small part of John Steinbeck's EAST OF EDEN has been used in the motion picture version of it that Elia Kazan has done, and it is questionable whether that part contains the best of the book...But the stubborn fact is that the people who move about in the film are not sufficiently well established to give point to the anguish through which they go, and the demonstrations of their torment are perceptibly stylized and grotesque. Especially is this true of James Dean in the role of Cal...He scuffs his feet, he whirls, he pouts, he sputters, he leans against walls, he rolls his eyes, he swallows his words, he ambles slack-kneed—all like Marlon Brando used to do...Whatever there might be of reasonable torment in this youngster is buried beneath the clumsy display." —Bosley Crowther

HOLLYWOOD REPORTER: "The box office asset of a handsome and dynamic young actor named James Dean. This is the boy who is apt to captivate the typical movie fans whether or not they like tragic stories. He is that rare thing, a young actor who is a great actor, and the troubled eloquence with which he puts over the problems of misunderstood youth may lead to his being accepted by young audiences as a sort of symbol of their generation. He's the only actor I've seen who'd be completely right for Romeo...If this film is to reap the profits it deserves no time should be lost in giving him a big fan magazine build-up, not because he is trivial, but because it's the quickest way to rally people to his support." —Jack Moffit

HOLLYWOOD REPORTER: "Jimmy Dean, bespectacled and blue-jeaned, driving down the Hollywood Boulevard, gaping at the EAST OF EDEN waiting lines—a nightly routine with the flabbergasted young star."

VARIETY: "Much pro and con probably will develop about James Dean, unknown to whom Kazan gave a full scale introduction. It is no credit to Kazan that Dean seems required to play his lead character as though he were straight out of a Marlon Brando mold. Just how flexible his talent is will have to be judged on other screen roles, although he has a basic appeal that manages to get through to the viewer despite the heavy burden of carboning another's acting style in voice and mannerisms. It should be interesting to see what he can do as Dean." (February 15, 1955).

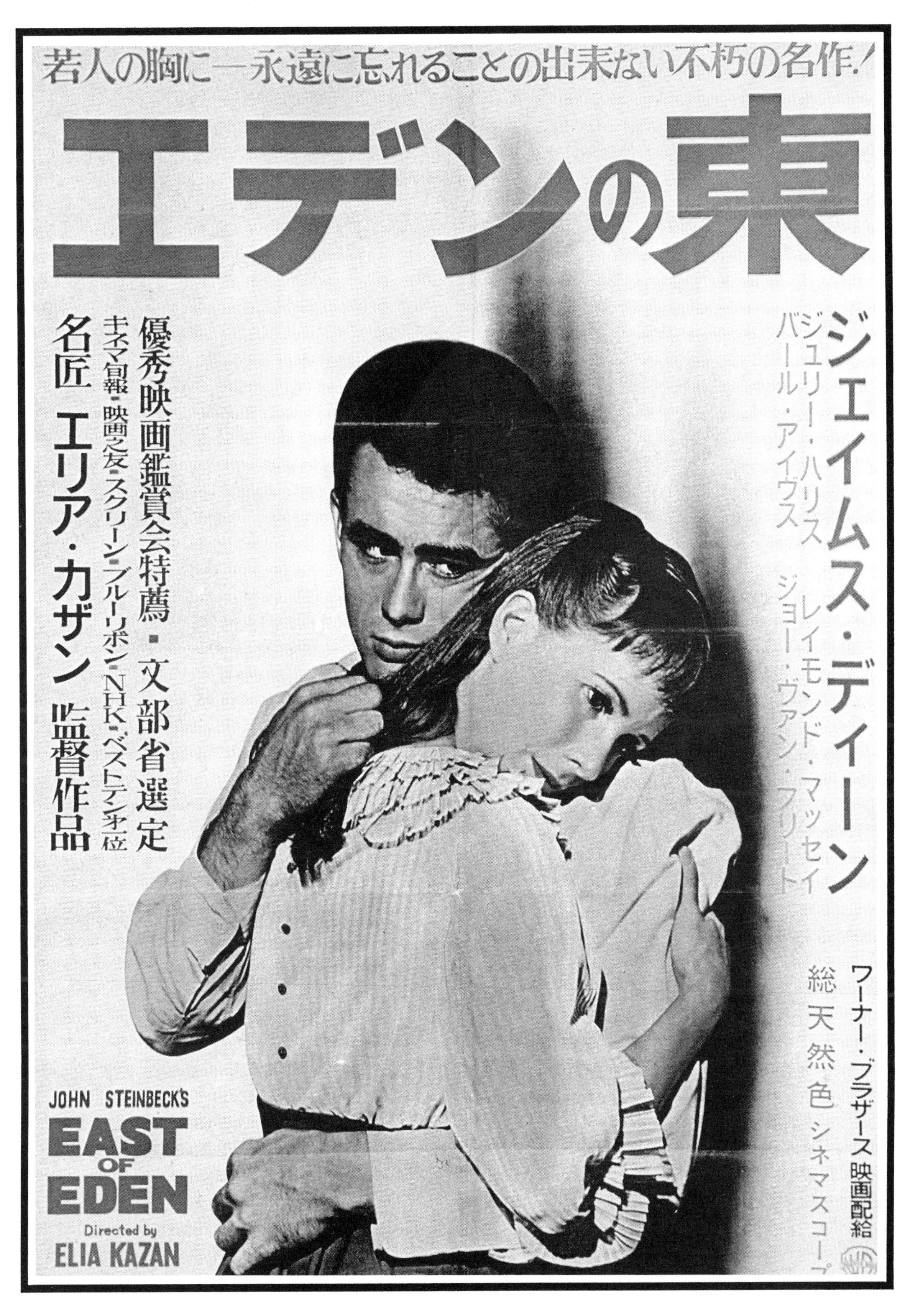

Japanese movie poster.

Movie poster.

Ratings

Maltin: ****

Scheuer: ***1/2

Martin/Porter: *****

Motion Picture Guide: ****

Rebel Without a Cause

Warner Bros., 1955

CREDITS

CAST

Jim Stark (James Dean); Judy (Natalie Wood); Plato (Sal Mineo); Jim's father (Jim Backus); Jim's mother (Ann Doran); Buzz (Corey Allen); Judy's father (William Hopper); Judy's mother (Rochelle Hudson); Jim's grandmother (Virginia Brissac); Moose (Nick Adams); Goon (Dennis Hopper); Cookie (Jack Simmons); Plato's maid (Marietta Canty); Chick (Jack Grinnage); Helen (Beverly Long); Mil (Steffi Sidney); Crunch (Frank Mazzola); Harry (Clifford Morris); Lecturer (Ian Wolfe); Juvenile Officer Ray (Edward Platt); Gene (Robert Foulk); Bean (Jimmy Baird); Guide (Dick Wessel); Sargeant (Nelson Leigh); Woman Officer (Louise Lane); Officer (House Peters); Attendant (Gus Schilling); Monitor (Bruce Noonan); Old Lady Teacher (Almira Sessions); Hoodlum (Peter Miller); Desk Sergeant (Paul Bryar); Police Chief (Paul Birch); Moose's father (Robert Williams); Church's father (David McMahon)

CREW

Directed by Nicolas Ray
Screenplay by Steward Stern
(adapted by Irving Shulman
from a story by Nicolas Ray)
Produced by David Weisbart
Music by Leonard Rosenman
Dir. of Photography: Ernest Haller
Art Director: Malcolm Bert
Edited by William Ziegler

Film Facts :

Premiere:

Premiere: Astor Theatre, New York, October 26, 1955.

Awards:

REBEL WITHOUT A CAUSE was banned until 1964 in Spain. When it was finally released, it won the Best Film of the Year award.

Other Film Facts

* Filming began on March 28, 1955 and was completed on May 25, 1955.

* REBEL WITHOUT A CAUSE cost $600,000 to produce.

* This film established Dean as the quintessential image of the restless 1950s youth generation.

* Adults were disturbed by this film, now a cult classic, stating that it advocated violence, death, madness, and indicted parents for committing sins against their spoiled offspring.

* Warner Brothers originally proposed that Tab Hunter and Jayne Mansfield play the leading roles that were eventually given to Dean and Wood.

* James Dean insisted on playing the fight scenes for real against the requests of crew and production staff members. He did nevertheless agree to wear a protective vest.

* This was Natalie Wood's first adult or near-adult role in movies. Previously, she had been a child star.

* This was Sal Mineo's film debut.

* Both Natalie Wood and Sal Mineo received Academy Award nominations for their performances in REBEL WITHOUT A CAUSE.

* Dean parodies 'Mr. Magoo' (Jim Backus' character) in the scene around the empty swimming pool at the deserted mansion.

* The mansion originally belonged to J. Paul Getty and was rented at $200 a day for the filming of scenes in REBEL. The same house appeared in the movie SUNSET BOULEVARD. Now torn down, the house originally was on Wilshire Boulevard and Crenshaw Avenue.

* Dean actually broke two bones in his hand when he hit the desk in Juvenile Officer Ray's office.

* This film covers a 24-hour period and was changed from the original Christmas time to Easter.

* Locations used in this movie included Santa Monica Community College, the Hollywood jail, and the D.W. Griffith Observatory and Planetarium. James Dean was not new to two of these locations.

Five years before he had attended Santa Monica Community College and he had made a soft drink commercial at Griffith Park. Today, there is a monument at Griffith Observatory honoring James Dean.

* Some movies have been categorized as "jinxed" because of the ill-fated turn of events which later befell their major stars. REBEL WITHOUT A CAUSE must surely rank as one of these movies. Beginning with the tragic death of James Dean in an automobile accident in 1955, even before the picture was released, several REBEL cast members have been victims of tragic deaths. Nick Adams (Moose) was found dead of a drug overdose in 1976; Sal Mineo (Plato) was murdered outside of his West Hollywood apartment in 1978; William Hopper (Judy's father), Ed Platt (Officer Ray), and Nicolas Ray (Director) all died from natural causes; Pier Angeli (Dean's girlfriend) was a victim of an overdose of drugs; and the most recent victim was Natalie Wood, who drowned in the waters off Catalina in 1981.

A scene from Rebel.

THE STORY....

A man beaten up by some teen-age toughs is left lying unconscious in the street. Jim Stark, a troublemaker when the viewer sees him for the first time, is an unruly youth questioned by the police and then released for lack of evidence. Before his release, he reveals a disrespect for his domineering mother and weakling father, who smother him at home with their artificial love.

Jim's troublesome ways have caused his family to move repeatedly until they settled in Los Angeles. With Judy, a young girl who turns him down for a date, and his pal Plato, a disturbed rich kid, Jim tries to join a gang led by Buzz. Instead, Jim and Buzz wind up fighting a knife duel and agree to meet later for a test whereby the boys each get into a hot rod, drive the cars toward the edge of a cliff, and leap out seconds before the vehicles tumble to the jagged rocks below.

Both boys race at breakneck speed, the cliff's edge looming ever nearer. Buzz reaches for the door, but his jacket sleeve hooks over the handle. Trapped, he and the car spin through the air to a violent end below.

Fearing Jim will go to the police, Buzz's friends track him to a deserted mansion where he, Judy, and Plato, armed with his father's gun, are hiding out. Plato opens fire, killing one of the youths. Summoned by the shots, police close in and order the gun-crazed youth to surrender.

Plato makes a furtive move which is mistaken by a policeman who fires at him. The officer's shot kills Plato.

Jim, saddened by his buddy's death, is comforted by his parents. Jim weeps for the misguided boy dead in his arms as his father finds the courage to stand up to his mother, and tells him that they will work things out.
Jim and Judy embrace. From this experience, they have come to understand one another.

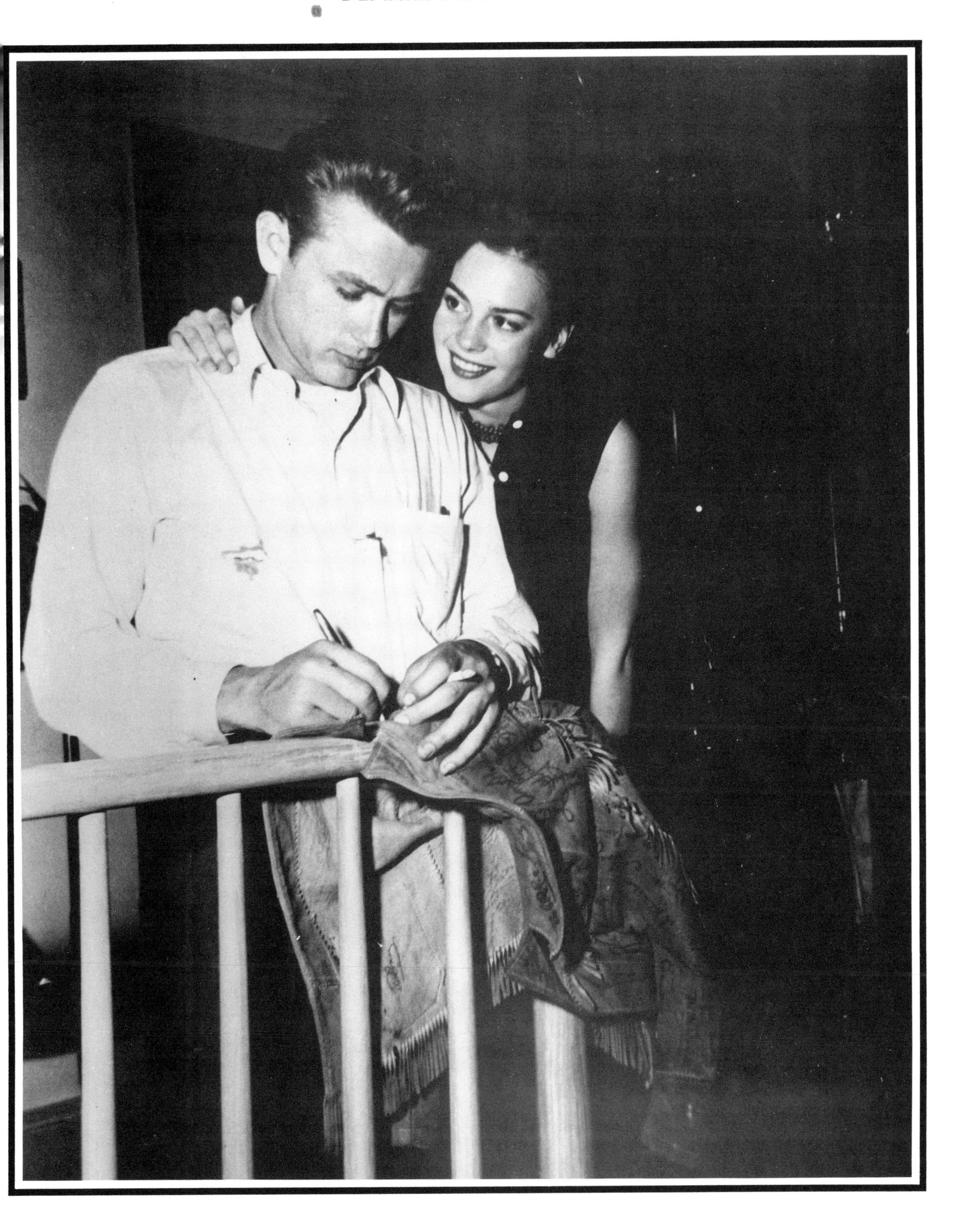

CinemaScope
JAMES
DEAN
REGIE: NICHOLAS RAY
WARNER COLOR
"Rebel
without
a Cause"

Rebel: The Critics

SATURDAY REVIEW: "The late James Dean reveals completely the talent latent in his EAST OF EDEN performance. As a new and unwilling member of the gang, a boy who recognized more clearly than any of the others his need for help, he projects the wildness, the torment, the crude tenderness of a rootless generation. Gone are the Brando mannerisms, gone the too-obvious Kazan touch. He stands out as a remarkable talent; and he was cut down by the same passions he exposes so tellingly in this strange and forceful picture."
—Arthur Knight

SUNDAY EXPRESS: "Again one is impressed by the effect of powerful emotion so harnessed and controlled that if it were not carefully rationed it would explode."
— Milton Schulman

NEWSWEEK: "In this movie, he wins an auto race with death. Only four weeks ago, at the age of twenty-four, he lost one."

AMERICA: "One of the film's chief exhibits of teen-age irresponsibility is a full dress demonstration of a game called 'chicken'...The tragic coincidence that Dean lost his life in an automobile accident a few weeks ago, gives this sequence an almost unbearable morbid ring."

NEW REPUBLIC: "It is significant that there is little interest in what Dean might have gone on to do if he had not died. His death was a fitting culmination to his life...senseless, but justified by the story. There was no future for Dean, just as there was no future for Bellow's, Gold's or Baldwin's characters. These contemporary heros are not the intellectual nihilists of Turgenev or Dostoevsky; they are rather the results of the naturalistic-existential schools of writing. In all instances they are without direction and aims, dominated by the utter helplessness of their positions and unwilling, or unable, to win even one victory."

NEW REPUBLIC went on to write:
"In REBEL WITHOUT A CAUSE, rebellion is made not against parents or law but against the universal conditions of life. The children do not rebel against the bad or the good, but against ALL. In search of love, they are acquitted of any breach of the law or morality. In James Dean, his movie roles, his life and death, there is a general lack of identity. He is supposedly like all the rest of us and to criticize him would be self-criticism."

Japanese movie poster.

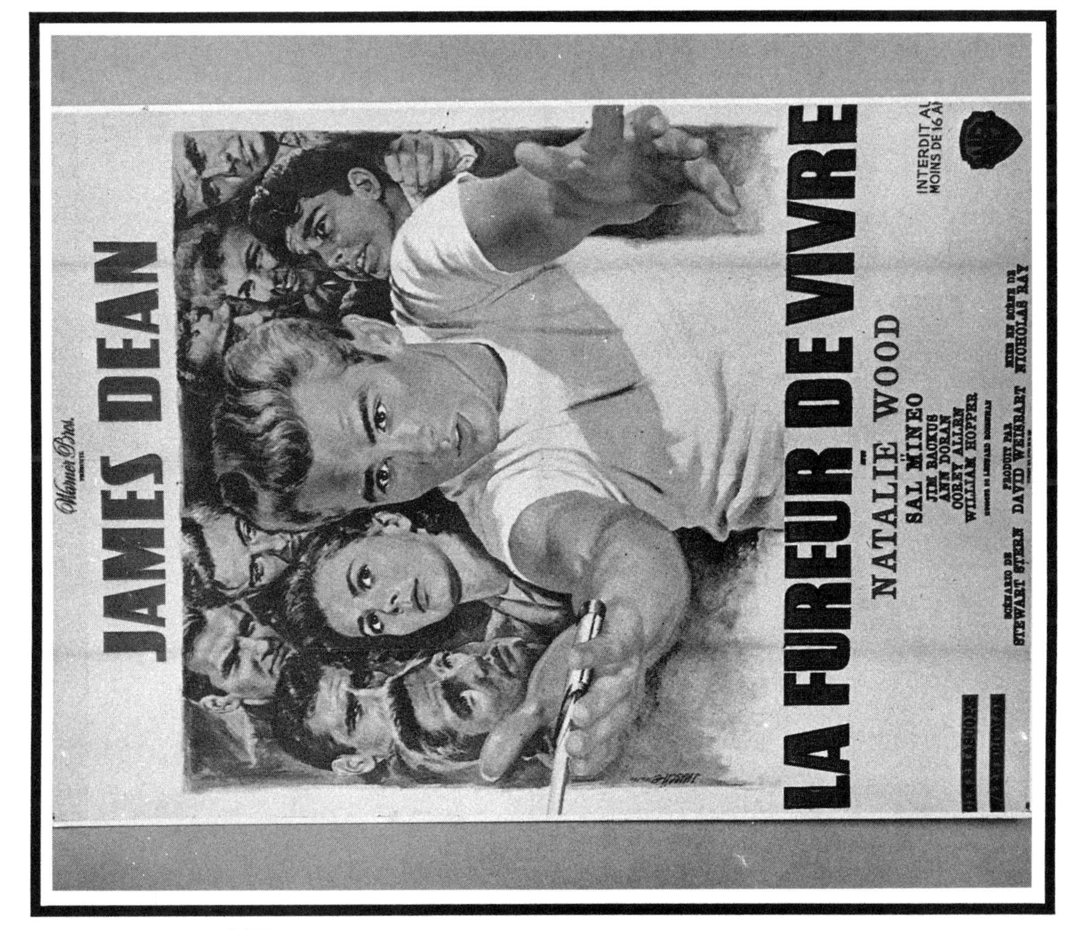

TOP: German movie poster.

BOTTOM: French movie poster.

NEW YORK HERALD TRIBUNE: "The movie is written and acted so ineptly, directed so sluggishly, that all names but one will be omitted here. The exception is Dean, the gifted young actor who was killed last month. His rare talent and appealing personality even shine through this turgid melodrama."
— William Zinsser

VARIETY: "The performance of the star, James Dean, will excite discussion especially in connection with irony of his own recent crash death under real-life conditions of recklessness, which form a press agent frame as the picture goes into release. In EAST OF EDEN under Elia Kazan's direction the twenty-four year-old actor was widely thought to be doing a Marlon Brando. But freed from Kazan's evaluations of character this resemblance vanishes. Almost free of mannerisms under Ray's pacing, Dean is very effective as a boy groping for adjustment to people. As a farewell performance he leaves behind, with this film, genuine artistic regret, for here was a talent which might have touched the heights."

DAILY TELEGRAPH: "Among several fine performances one is unforgettable in its subtlety and strength, the power to suggest by a shrug, an awkward gesture or hesitant word, an unexpectedly charming smile or suddenly unleashed fury all the loneliness of the young, their dreams and agonized confusions."
—Campbell Dixon

The reception committee for
the new kid on the block!

JAMES
DEAN

The overnight sensation of 'East of Eden'

Warner Bros. put
all the force of
the screen
into a challenging
drama of today's
juvenile violence!

"REBEL
WITHOUT
A CAUSE"

IN CINEMASCOPE
AND WARNERCOLOR

. . . and they both come
from 'good' families!

ALSO STARRING
NATALIE WOOD SAL MINEO · JIM BACKUS · ANN DORAN · COREY ALLEN · WILLIAM HOPPER · STEWART STERN DAVID WEISBART · NICHOLAS RAY

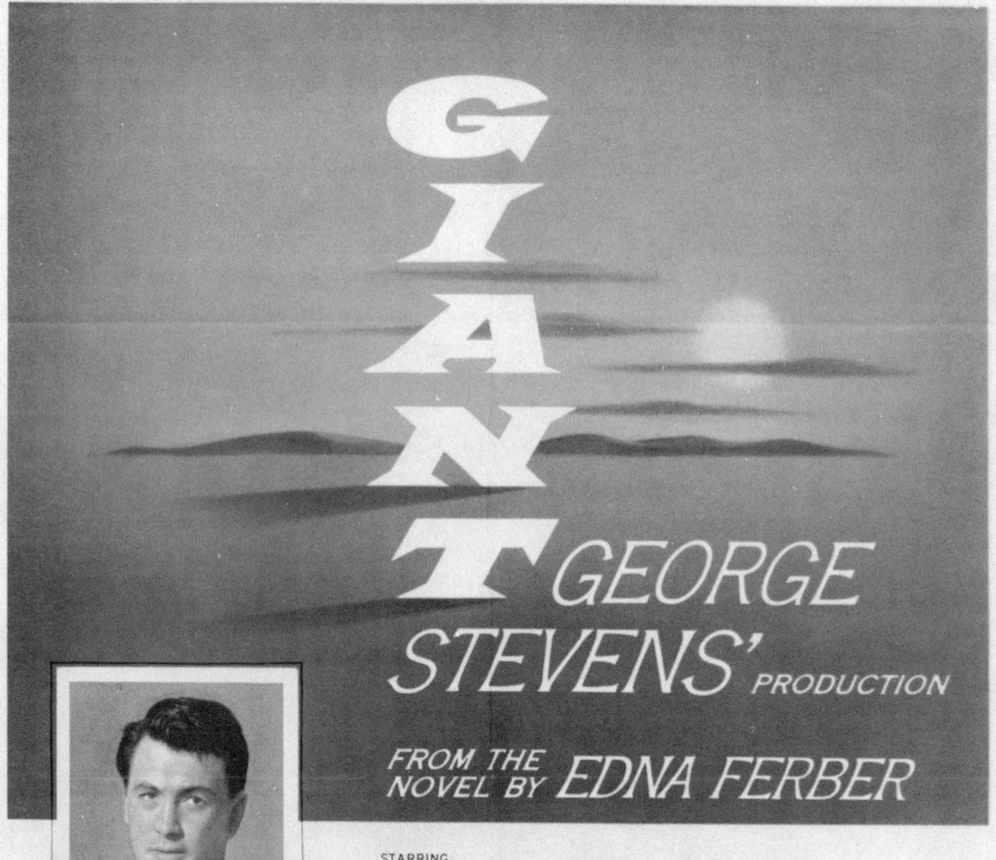
A PICTURE OF PROUD PEOPLE, A LOVE STORY, A CAVALCADE--A CONFLICT OF CREEDS--A PERSONAL DRAMA OF STRONG LONGINGS--A BIG STORY OF BIG THINGS AND BIG FEELINGS--- THIS IS 'GIANT'!
GIANT
GEORGE STEVENS' PRODUCTION
FROM THE NOVEL BY EDNA FERBER
STARRING
ELIZABETH TAYLOR
AS LESLIE LYNNTON...whether you loved her in the open, or hid it inside you--you hungered.
ROCK HUDSON
AS BICK BENEDICT...who was big enough to stand up and take what he wanted; and biggest, one day, when he crawled.
JAMES DEAN
AS JETT RINK...he was made of laughs and lies and loving looks; he was made to get to the top--so he could have the fun of falling all the way down.
PRESENTED BY WARNER BROS. IN WARNERCOLOR
AND PRESENTING
CARROLL BAKER
ALSO STARRING
JANE WITHERS · CHILL WILLS · MERCEDES McCAMBRIDGE
SAL MINEO
WITH DENNIS HOPPER · SCREEN PLAY BY FRED GUIOL AND IVAN MOFFAT
MUSIC COMPOSED AND CONDUCTED BY DIMITRI TIOMKIN
PRODUCED BY GEORGE STEVENS AND HENRY GINSBERG
DIRECTED BY GEORGE STEVENS
PRESENTED BY WARNER BROS.

Ratings

Maltin: ****

Scheuer: ***1/2

Martin/Porter: ***1/2

Motion Picture Guide: ****

Giant

Warner Bros., 1956

CREDITS

CAST

Leslie Lynnton Benedict (Elizabeth Taylor); Bick Benedict (Rock Hudson); Jett Rink (James Dean); Luz Benedict (Mercedes McCambridge); Uncle Bawley (Chill Wills); Vashti Synthe (Jane Withers); Pinky Synthe (Robert Nichols); Jordon Benedict III (Dennis Hopper); Juana (Elsa Cardenas); Judy Benedict (Fran Bennett); Luz Benedict II (Carroll Baker); Bob Benedict (Earl Holliman); Dr. Horace Lynnton (Paul Fix); Mrs. Horace Lynnton (Judith Evenlyn); Lacey Lynnton (Carolyn Craig); Sir David Karfrey (Rodney Taylor); Old Polo (Alexander Scourby); Angel Obregon II (Sal Mineo); Bale Clinch (Monte Hale); Adarene Clinch (Mary Ann Edwards); Swazey (Naopleon Whiting); Dr. Guerra (Maurice Jara); Whiteside (Charles Watts); Angel Obregon I (Victor Millan); Mrs. Obregon (Pilar Del Rey); Gomez (Felipe Turich); Gabe Target (Sheb Wolley); Mexican Priest (Francisco Villalobos); Watts (Ray Whitley); Lupe (Tina Manard); Petra (Ana Maria Majalca); Sarge (Mickey Simpson); Lona Lane (Noreen Nash); Harper (Guy Teague); Eusubio (Natividad Vacio); Dr. Walker (Max Terhune); Dr. Borneholm (Ray Bennett); Mary Lou Decker (Barbara Berie); Vern Decker (George Dunne); Clay Hodgins (Slim Talbor); Clay Hodgins Sr. (Tex Driscoll); Elsie Lou Hodgins (Juney Ellis)

CREW

Directed by George Stevens
Screenplay by Fred Guiol and Ivan Moffat from the novel by Edna Ferber
Produced by Henry Ginsberg and George Stevens
Music by Dimitri Tiomkin
Dir Photography: William C. Mellor
Art Director: Ralph Hurst
Edited by Fred Bohaman and Phil Anderson

Film Facts :

Premiere:

Premiere: November 10, 1956.

Awards:

* For the second time James Dean was nominated for an Academy Award as Best Performance. He had received the first in 1956 for his performance as Cal Trask in EAST OF EDEN. Ernest Borgnine won the Oscar for MARTY. Again, Dean was nominated for his role in GIANT and again, a living actor (Yul Brenner for KING AND I), received the award.

* GIANT received in total ten Academy Award nominations. Besides Dean, Rock Hudson and Mercedes McCambridge received nominations. Only George Stevens won an Oscar, his second.

* George Stevens originally had requested that the lead role go to Grace Kelly instead of Elizabeth Taylor.

Other Film Facts

* Filming began on May 18, 1955 (Dean joined the cast on June 3, 1955) and it was completed in late September 1955 with Dean's final day of filming on the 22nd of September. He was invited to a showing of the rushes of the 'last supper' scene on September 27, 1955. In characteristic fashion, he arrived late for the showing; this was to be the last time he and George Stevens would talk. Dean told Stevens, "Now it's all over, we don't have to bug each other no more."

* GIANT was filmed in Marfa, Texas, a city of approximately 2900 people located 60 miles from the Mexican border and three hours by car from El Paso.

* The Victorian mansion used in GIANT was built in Hollywood at a cost of approximately $200,000 and ship in sections to Texas. After filming, it remained on the land and was eventually converted into a hay barn.

* Over 600,000 feet of film were shot while filming GIANT; in the end only 25,000 feet were actually used.

* Dean's salary for GIANT was set at $15,000. However with overtime he actually received more than $30,000.

* In the final scene, Dean (Jett Rink) is supposed to make a speech. Dean made the speech, however, it was totally incoherent. Rumor has it that it was later dubbed by an "anonymous" actor, reportedly, Nick Adams.

* The press book prepared by Warner Brothers for GIANT made absolutely no mention of Dean's death. It would have been impossible to discover that James Dean was dead from materials provided in the press book.

* Alan Ladd and Richard Burton were both rumored to have been considered for the role of Jett Rink.

* GIANT grossed more than 12 million dollars the first time around.

* During the filming of GIANT Dean was asked to do a commercial for the National Highway Committee. The irony in this commercial is obvious. While visiting with Gig Young, Dean discusses his love for racing and then concludes the commercial with the following prophetic warning: "Remember, drive safely because the life you save may be mine."

* At the conclusion of GIANT, Jane Deacy, Dean's agent, came to Hollywood to negotiate a new contract for him. This new contract guaranteed him one million dollars over the next six years, with three months each year of free time to do what he wished.

"The Crucifixion"

THE STORY....

Bick Benedict, the young owner of a half-million-acre cattle ranch in Texas, comes to Maryland to buy a magnificent black stallion. He meets, falls in love with and quickly marries Leslie.

Though they are much in love, there are many clashes of temperament at their vast Reata Ranch, so different from Leslie's home in Maryland. Leslie is shocked at the status of the Mexican ranch hands who are underpaid and underprivileged. She takes matters into her own hands by giving them medical care.

A stubborn spinster, Bick's sister, Luz, runs the house. Her unreasonable rule over the Reata Ranchi is ended when she is killed in a riding accident. Her loathing of Bick and Leslie lingers bitterly in the form of her will in which she bequeaths a small part of Reata to Jett Rink, a violent young ranch hand who continuously quarrels with Bick while dreaming of the day he will make his own million.

He is convinced that his new property is the beginning of his new fortune and his dreams will soon come true. He strikes oil and goes on to great riches. Leslie and Bick have three children who, when grown up, all go against the wishes of their parents.

Their son, Jody, announces his marriage to Juana, a beautiful Mexican girl who is studying medicine. Bick is dismayed at the idea of having a Mexican girl as Mrs. Jordan Benedict III.

Reluctantly, all the Benedicts accept an invitation to the elaborate opening of the new hotel owned by the now fabulously wealthy Jett Rink. Bick is furious to discover his daughter Luz as Queen of Jett's spectacular model parade.

When Juana is refused service in the beauty salon of the hotel, an enraged Jody looks for Jett, whom he considers responsible for the insult to his wife. He finds him in the banquet room as Jett is about to deliver his dedication speech. Before Jody can land a punch, two henchmen pin his arms back while Jett knocks him out. Bick challenges Jett to a fight outside, but Jett is so drunk and helpless that Bick leaves him in disgust. Later, Jett passes out cold on the speaker's dais before he can deliver his speech.

Young Luz is angry at Jody for the way she thinks they have disgraced the family and ruined Jett's big evening and goes to the darkened banquet room where the still drunk Jett is delivering his speech to an empty room. Completely disillusioned, Luz returns to her parents.

Bick and his family drive to Reata. In a mood of relief and good cheer, they stop by a diner on the highway. A burly young man eyes Luz with distaste, and shortly afterwards orders some impoverished Mexican travellers out.

Bick fights him but is no match for the much younger man and ends up on the floor. Back at Reata, Bick grumbles to Leslie that he has been a failure, that nothing has worked out as he planned it. In Leslie's eyes, Bick was at last fighting for fundamental justice and she yells at him: "After a hundred years, the Benedict family is a real success."

JAMES DEAN
GEORGE
STEVENS'
PRODUCTION
GIANT
FROM THE NOVEL BY
EDNA FERBER
STARRING
ELIZABETH TAYLOR
ROCK HUDSON
JAMES DEAN

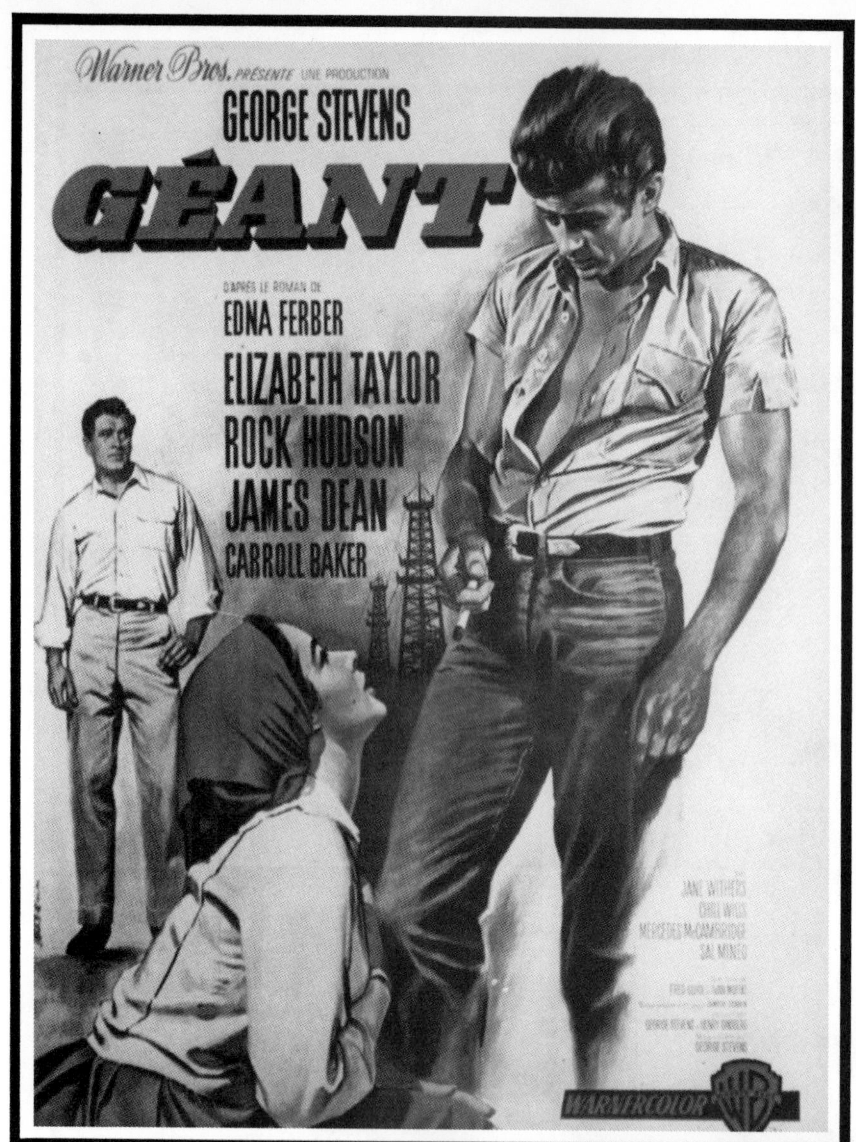

LEFT: French movie poster.

大テキサス三十年の自然と人間の激動のなかに美しく描き出された愛の叙事詩!
ジャイアンツ
エリザベス・テーラー/ジェームス・ディーン/ロック・ハドスン主演
原作 エドナ・ファーバー
撮影 ウイリアム・C・メラー
音楽 ディミトリー・ティオムキン
GIANT
総天然色
WB

Giant: The Critics

NEW YORK TIMES: "It is the late James Dean who makes this malignant role the most tangy and corrosive in the film. Mr. Dean plays this curious villain with a stylized spookiness—a sly sort of off-beat languor and slur of language—that concentrates spite. This is a haunting cap-stone to the brief career of Mr. Dean."
— Bosley Crowther.

FILMS IN REVIEW. "...[Taylor's] scenes with an off-hand ranch-hand were ...rendered pointless by James Dean's one and only successful acting style—the loutish and malicious petulance which present-day teenagers profess to admire. Dean made the young Jett Rink such a boor not even a wife more neurotic than the one Miss Taylor was portraying could have thought him attractive.
"Since Dean is dead I shall say nothing about his attempt to portray the mature Jett Rink, except to say it is embarrassing to see."
— Courtland Phipps.

TIME: "James Dean who was killed in a sports car crash two weeks after his last scene in GIANT was shot, in this film clearly shows for the first (and fatefully the last) time what his admirers always said he had: a streak of genius. He has caught the Texas accent to nasal perfection, and mastered that lock-hipped, high-heeled, stagger of the wrangler, and the wry little jerks and smirks, tics and twitches, grunts and giggles that make up most of the language of a man who talks to himself a good deal more than he does to anyone else. In one scene, indeed, in a long drunken mumble with actress Carroll Baker...Dean is able to press an amazing array of subtleties into the mood of the movement, to achieve what is certainly the finest piece of atmosphere acting seen on the screen since Marlon Brando and Rod Steiger did their 'brother' scene in ON THE WATERFRONT."

VARIETY (October 18, 1956): "...In the light of the current death cult starring the late James Dean it's probably safe to assume that he'll be the strongest draw on the GIANT marquee. No one should be disappointed, and the film only proves what a promising talent has been lost. As the shiftless, envious, bitter ranchhand who hates society, Dean delivers an outstanding portrayal. Plenty of screentime is devoted to him, and he makes the most of the juicy role. Whether in his scenes with Miss Taylor, whom he admires, or as the oil tycoon who shows up at a banquet in his honor in a drunken stupor, Dean is believable. It's a socko performance..."

Japanese movie poster.

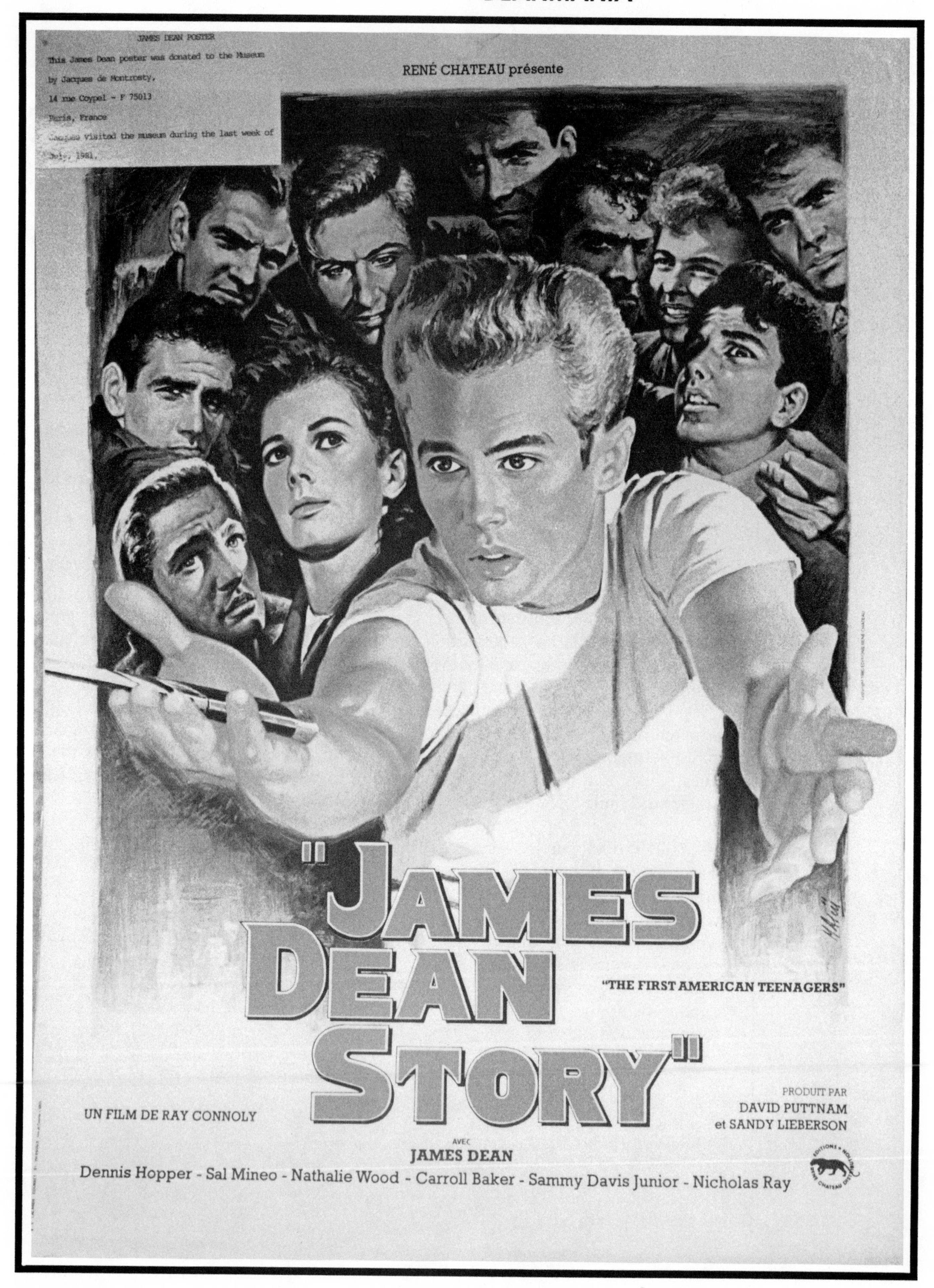
JAMES DEAN POSTER

This James Dean poster was donated to the Museum by Jacques de Montrosty, 14 rue Coypel - F 75013 Paris, France

Jacques visited the museum during the last week of July, 1981.

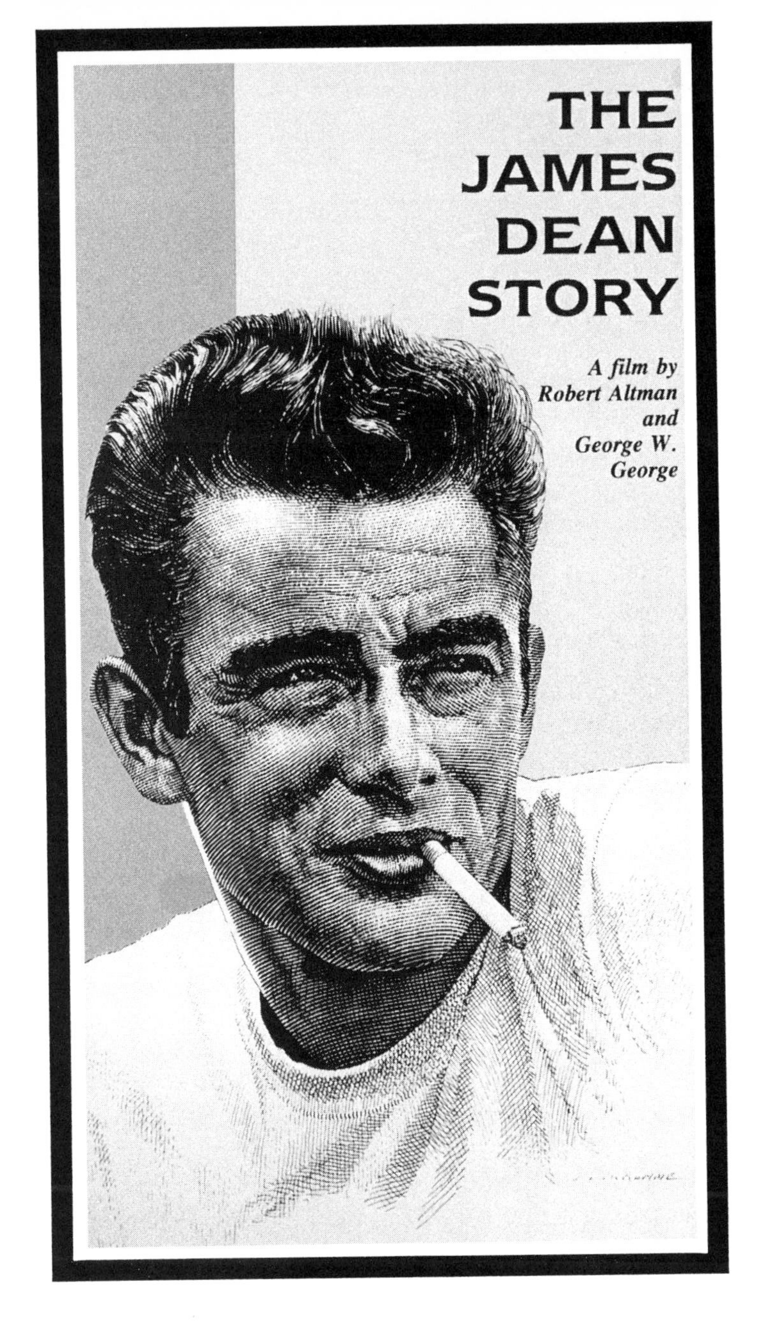

The James Dean Story

Warner Bros., 1957

CREDITS

CAST
Most of Dean's close friends avoided taking part in this production. However, his aunt and uncle, Mr. and Mrs. Marcus Winslow and his paternal grandparents, Mr. and Mrs. Charlie Dean were convinced to take part. Other cast members include Hollywood contemporaries, former girl-friends, and acquaintances of Dean's both in Hollywood and New York.

CREW
Directed by Robert Altman
Produced by Robert Altman and George W. George
Written by Stewart Stern

Film Facts :

Premiere:

Released in New York in 1957

Other Film Facts

* Originally an actor (Robert Conrad) was considered to play the part of James Dean. Fortunately, reason prevailed and this idea was dropped in favor of James Dean playing "himself".

* The film contains interviews, rare footage of Dean's television and film performances, pictures, and an occasional remark or two by those who knew Dean.

* The film failed miserably; was ignored by fans; and was quickly withdrawn from theatre circuits by Warner Brothers. It is now available both on videotape and laser disk

THE STORY....

A biographical documentary presented by Producer/Director Robert Altman. This film, 80 minutes in length, explores the personal life, the moments of James Dean's life between films. With commentary provided by Stewart Stern, the film features never-before-seen footage from EAST OF EDEN , the National Highway Committee public safety message and rare film from the Hollywood premiere of GIANT.

Album cover from record based on motion picture soundtrack.

The Critics...

NEW YORK TIMES (October 19, 1957): "What should be an effective contribution to the perpetuation of the legend of the late James Dean is achieved in THE JAMES DEAN STORY, which was added to the bill at the Paramount yesterday [October 18, 1957]. Intimations of immortality run all through it. It should be irresistible to the Dean fans.

This eighty-two minute memorial to the 24-year-old movie actor who was killed in an automobile accident in California in 1955 is made up of photographs, film clips, reenactments and interviews with relatives and friends, edited into a sort of cinematic elegy, with a commentary that throbs with deep laments.

Obviously it is angled to the audience that found in young Dean a symbol and sanctuary for the self-pity and self-dramatization of youth. It says he was wracked with doubts and torments, nursed a childish belief that he was 'bad' and did reckless things as rebellion against the insecurity and loneliness of his soul.

...at one point, the narrator (Martin Gabel) says, 'He remembered the ocean and the sea gull in flight and he knew he had found his power.'...Mr. Gabel [goes on to say], 'For the first time, he [Dean] found the timid belief that life was possible.'

Apparently, the people who made this picture were not sure when Dean 'arrived.' 'He prowled through the night like a hunter' is the endless threnody.

Several people who knew the young actor appear simply and with genuine dignity to say some plain things about him..."—Bosley Crowther

初めての出あい。
風が吹く。閃光が走る。
いま、聞こえてくる——
ジーンズ、ポルシェ、ノンストップ
青春のきらめき。
ジミー、君は生きている。
JAMES DEAN
THE
FIRST AMERICAN
TEENAGER
●貴重な未公開フィルムでつづるジミーの新たなるプロフィール!
青春よ
ジェームズ・ディーンのすべて
永遠に
製作デビッド・プトナム/サンディ・リーバーソン
監督レイ・コノリー
デニス・ホッパー
ナタリー・ウッド
レスリー・キャロン
サミー・デイビス・Jr
キャロル・ベイカー
サル・ミネオ
リー・ストラスバーグ
ニコラス・レイ
ナレーター
ステーシー・キーチ
東宝東和提供/カラー作品/アメリカ映画
映倫

James Dean: First American Teenager

ZIV, 1975

CREDITS

CAST
Corey Allen, Carroll Baker, Leslie Caron, Sammy Davis, Jr., Dennis Hopper, Kenneth Kendall, Jack Larson, Sal Mineo, Adeline Nall, Maila Nurmi, Jean Owen, Hal Owen, Nicholas Ray, Leonard Rosenman, Capt. E. Tripke, Cristine White, Peter Witt and Natalie Wood.

CREW
Director: Ray Connolly
Producers: David Puttman, Sandy Lieberson
Editor: Peter Hollywood
Photography by: Peter Hannan, Mike Molloy, Robert Gersikoff
Narrated by: Stacy Keach

THE STORY....

A provocative, revealing portrait of the first cult hero of our time. Viewers will find rare footage, never seen before, of James Dean who wished to experience all that life had to offer and then applied this to his life and his work.

Personal reflections of various stars including Elizabeth Taylor, Rock Hudson, Sammy Davis Jr., Natalie Wood, Sal Mineo, Christine White, Carroll Baker and others provide viewers with tremendous insight into the character and person, James Dean.

The film features music by David Bowie, Eric Clapton, Neil Sedaka, Elton John and the Eagles, which further reveals the incredible impact that James Dean has had on the American culture.

This is truly the most personable, intimate look at one of America's truly great film legends, who lived fast, died young, and left America a legacy to live by.

The Critics...

LOS ANGELES TIMES (June 6, 1976): "...earnest, fairly comprehensive, occasionally superficial and evasive documentary that includes generous portions of the three films he completed before his death in 1955 in a car crash at the age of 24.
"The quality that makes an actor a star is perhaps inevitably finally elusive, but Dean projected a vulnerability combined with an intense magnetism that held his generation in thrall...documentarian Ray Connolly has rounded up plenty of people who knew him well enough to offer some insight into what made him tick. (There are some intriguing absences, however, beginning with EAST OF EDEN's' director, Eliz Kazan.)
"The impression we receive, one that confirms what most people already have, is that of a young man of more talent than discipline, with much ambition and many insecurities, possessed of both a gift for self-dramatization and a streak of self-destructiveness..." —Kevin Thomas

NEW YORK POST (November 19, 1976): "JAMES DEAN—THE FIRST AMERICAN TEENAGER... is a documentary about the legendary cult hero whose survival for these 21 years after death may seem mysterious to some. They need wonder no longer, for this picture, drawing material from his three biggest films, EAST OF EDEN, REBEL WITHOUT A CAUSE and GIANT as well as his first screen test for Elia Kazan, and clips from four television plays, a road safety commercial, ironically, and a newsreel of him in his racing car, repeats his magical effect...
"This is a picture you should see if Jimmy Dean means anything at all to you, pro or con. Ray Connolly put it together. David Puttman and Sandy Lieberson produced it..."—Archer Winsten

VARIETY (September 16, 1975): "...Going for it is obviously painstaking research by British director-writer Ray Connolly, who unearthed footage from a number of early '50s Dean teleplays, his screentest for Elia Kazan, a road-safety commercial made, ironically, shortly before actor's fatal car crash, plus numerous little-seen stills and abundant clips from the three Warner pix, EAST OF EDEN, REBEL WITHOUT A CAUSE, and GIANT. Also contributing to the Dean mystique are interviews with guys and gals who were personally or professionally close to Dean—or as close as the introverted actor allowed them to be. But what remains most in favor is the fascination of Dean himself, everything about him working towards his cult glorification, which this pic is likely to further even more, or where forgotten, rekindle.
"For the pic points out, Dean is still amazingly topical, the precursor and still number one exponent of the secret American youth drama, the 'liberator' who gave the teenager his status.
"All in all, it's compulsive stuff for the buff, neatly edited (Peter Hollywood), written (Connolly) and commented (Stacy Keach) in as objective and unscyophantic a manner as possible. In no ways a whitewash, there are some eloquently descriptive quotes from people who know him of some of his non-conformist bits of bravura. One has the feeling that the myth would have survived even a more severe lambasting.
"What continues to amaze, as a lingering impression, is how little the Dean material—and indeed image—has aged (Dean died exactly 20 years ago). Not incidentally, pic also makes an appetite—whetting trailer for Dean's films, notably GIANT.
"Technically, it's a superior job, with a musical track (Elton John, David Bowie, The Eagles) which aptly fits material."

NOTE: This videotape is a copy of the original THE JAMES DEAN STORY

James Dean

HVL, 1988

James Dean

William Bast Productions, 1976

CREDITS

CAST
James Dean (Stephen McHattie); Bill Bast (Michael Brandon); Chris White (Candy Clark); Dizzy Sheridan (Meg Foster); Reva Randall (Jayne Meadows); Claire Folger (Katherine Helmond); Jan (Heather Menzies); Arlene (Leland Palmer); Norma Jean (Amy Irving); Psychiatrist (Robert Foxworth); Secretary (Chris White); Beverly (Brooke Adams); Ray (Julian Burton); Mechanic (Robert Kenton); Judge (Judge Murdock); Mr. Robbins (James O'Connell).

CREW
Directed by Robert Butler
Executive Producers:
Gerald I. Isenberg
and Gerald W. Abrams
Produced by
John Forbes and William Bast
Teleplay by William Bast
Photography: Frank Stanley
Edited by John A. Martinelli
Music by Billy Goldenberg
Art Directed by Perry Ferguson, II

Film Facts :

Premiere:

Premiere: NBC, February 19, 1976

Other Film Facts:

* This was a made-for-television movie lasting approximately 120 minutes.

* The story is based upon William Bast's biography of James Dean, JAMES DEAN A BIOGRAPHY (1956), the first to appear after Dean's death.

THE STORY....

An unusual presentation of the period of time during which James Dean and William Bast were roommates, students, and aspiring actors in the early 1950s in California.

"A glimpse into the psychology of fandom, this tape is a probing, oddly respectful look at people deeply moved by the spirit of James Dean. These otherwise everyday folks never got over the fateful day of September 30, 1955, despite the fact that many of them weren't even alive at the time...These people's sense of self was somehow irreversibly touched by image of the misunderstood rebel without a cause..."

-- Video Review, July 1989

Remembering James Dean

Mary Ann Michna, 1989

CREDITS

CAST
James Dean Fans

CREW
Directed and Produced by Mary Ann Michna

Film Facts :

* First place winner in "The Great Video Review Shootoff 1989"

* This was Mary Ann Michna's first video production. She bought her Sony CCD-V5 camcorder specifically to shoot this program.

* Michna has agreed to work with The James Dean Gallery to produce and direct future videotapes which will record pilgrimages to James Dean's hometown.

THE STORY....

REMEMBERING JAMES DEAN is a sometimes poignant and always fascinating look at Dean devotees and their visits to Dean's hometown of Fairmount, Indiana. If you're imagining a sarcastic documentary on fanatical pop-demigod worshippers, forget it. Michna treated her subjects with a delicate balance of respect and curiosity, her camera acting as an observer rather than inquisitor. "I didn't start out as a James Dean fan," Michna says. "I didn't know that the memorial existed until a friend took me. But there was something almost mystical about the place, the people who visited were so sincere and reverential that I got caught up in it myself."

The Critics...

VIDEO REVIEW (July, 1989): "In documentary style, Michna managed to coax truly unaffected reminiscences from her surprisingly candid interviewees—ranging from a trivia collector to Dean's high school biology teacher, who discusses Dean's involvement in 4H! Content to record her material rather than try to manipulate it, she achieved a level of insight and honesty that was truly fascinating."

James Dean on TV and Stage

(compiled with the assistance of Robert Rees, Dean video specialist and private collector)

TELEVISION

1950
'Pepsi-Cola' Commercial (some biographers list this as a commercial for 'Coca-Cola'. This commercial, one and one-half minutes in length, was filmed in Griffith Park. Dean, along with two future "Rebel" stars Nick Adams and Beverly Long participated in this commercial and would ironically return here later to film "Rebel Without a Cause." Dean received $30.00 for this commercial.)

1951
"Hill Number One" (plays John the Apostle. After his performance several girls at a local Catholic school formed the 'Immaculate Heart James Dean Appreciation Society', the first James Dean fan club.)

Bit parts in:
"Fixed Bayonets" (one line "it's a rear guard coming back" is later cut out.)
"Sailor Beware" (a Martin and Lewis film).
"Trouble Along the Way" (John Wayne also appears in this movie).
"Beat the Clock" (tested stunts to be performed by contestants on the show)

1952
US Steel Hour "Prologue to Glory"

Bit part
"Has Anybody Seen My Gal" (with Rock Hudson)

1953
Kate Smith Hour "Hound of Heaven"
Treasury-Men in Action "The Case of the Watchful Dog"
Treasury-Men in Action "The Case of the Sawed-off Shotgun"
Campbell Sound Stage "Something for an Empty Briefcase"
Campbell Sound Stage "Life Sentence"
Armstrong Circle Theatre "The Bells of Cockaigne"
Danger "No Room"
Danger "The Little Women"
Danger "Death is My Neighbor" (with Betsy Palmer)
Kraft Theatre "Keep Our Honor Bright"
Kraft Theatre "A Long Time Till Dawn" (written by Rod Serling)
US Steel Hour "The Thief"
Studio One Summer Theatre "Sentence of Death"
Johnson's Wax Program "Harvest"

1954
General Electric Theatre "I Am a Fool" (with Natalie Wood)
General Electric Theatre "The Dark, Dark Hours" (with Ronald Reagan)
Danger "Padlocks"
Philco TV Playhouse "Run Like a Thief"

1955
Schlitz Playhouse "The Unlighted Road"
US Steel Hour "The Thief" (with Mary Astor)

THEATRE

In addition to television appearances, James Dean appeared in two theatrical performances.
"See The Jaguar" premiered December 3rd, 1952. Dean played Willie Wilkins. The play closed three days after opening.
"The Immoralist" premiered February 8th, 1954. Dean played Bachir and after only two weeks he gave notice. Two weeks later he was signed by Kazan to play in EAST OF EDEN .

James Dean in "The Unlighted Road" from SCHLITZ PLAYHOUSE

One thing the rebel was never without
ORE PEOPLE RELY ON CHAMPION THAN ANY OTHER SPARK PLUG IN THE WORL
CHAMPION

Courtesy Maxine Rowland/Ohio

National Highway Safety Commercial...

PHOTO TOP OPPOSITE PAGE:

During the filming of GIANT James Dean took part in a thirty-second commercial for the National Highway Safety Committee. Dressed in his GIANT outfit, he talked with Gig Young.

Gig Young:

How fast does your car go?

Jimmy:

Oh, about a hundred miles per hour, clocked.

Gig Young:

You've used it to race, haven't you?

Jimmy:

Oh, one or two times.

Gig Young: Where?

Jimmy:

Oh, I showed pretty good at Palm Springs. I ran in a basic heat. People say racing is dangerous, but I'd rather take my chances on the track any day than on the highway...Well, Gig, I think I'd better take off.

(As Jim leaves he turns and says to Gig Young)

Jimmy:

And remember—drive safely—because the life you save may be MINE.

James Dean Awards and Honors

For his performance in "The Immoralist" James Dean received (1) The Antoinette Perry "Tony" award and (2) the Daniel Blum award—both for outstanding young actor of the year.

Dean was nominated twice for an Oscar for Best Actor for his performances in EAST OF EDEN and GIANT. Unfortunately, the 1955 award went to Ernest Borgnine and the 1956 award was won by Yul Brenner. Dean however rem ains the first actor to receive two nominations posthumously.

After Dean's death fan clubs were instrumental in securing the following awards for him:

* Best Actor of 1955, PHOTOPLAY magazine

* Special Achievement Medal, MODERN SCREEN magazine

* World's Favorite Actor by Hollywood Foreign Press Association

* Best Actor Award, Motion Picture Exhibitors

* Best Performance of the Year, Council of Motion Picture Organizations

* Filmdom's Famous Five Award (twice)

* Hall of Fame, Princeton University Foreign Film Awards include:

* Cinema Academy of France

* The Crystal Star; The Winged Victory Award, France

* The Academy Award, England

* Million Pearl Award, Japan

* Elokvva Journalist Statuette, Finland

* Cine-Revere Diploma, Belgium

Maila Nurmi, a Hollywood friend of Dean's, is reported to have given Dean a replica or an original Oscar (supposedly stolen from Frank Sinatra).which bore the engraving: "to James Dean for the best performance in Googies 1955"

There is nothing much deader than a dead motion picture actor, and yet,
even after James Dean had been some years dead,
when they filed out of the close darkness and the breathed-out air of the second and third and fourth run motion picture theaters
where they'd been seeing James Dean's old films, they still lined up:
the boys in the jackboots and the leather jackets,
the boys in the skintight jeans,
the boys in the broad motorbike belts,
before the mirrors in the restroom
to look at themselves
and see
James Dean;
the resentful hair,
the deep eyes floating in lonesomeness,
the bitter beat look,
the scorn on the lip.
Their pocket combs were out; they tousled up their hair and patted it down just so;
made big eyes at their eyes in the mirror,
pouted their lips in a sneer,
lost cats in love with themselves just like James Dean.

—John Dos Passos, Esquire, 1958

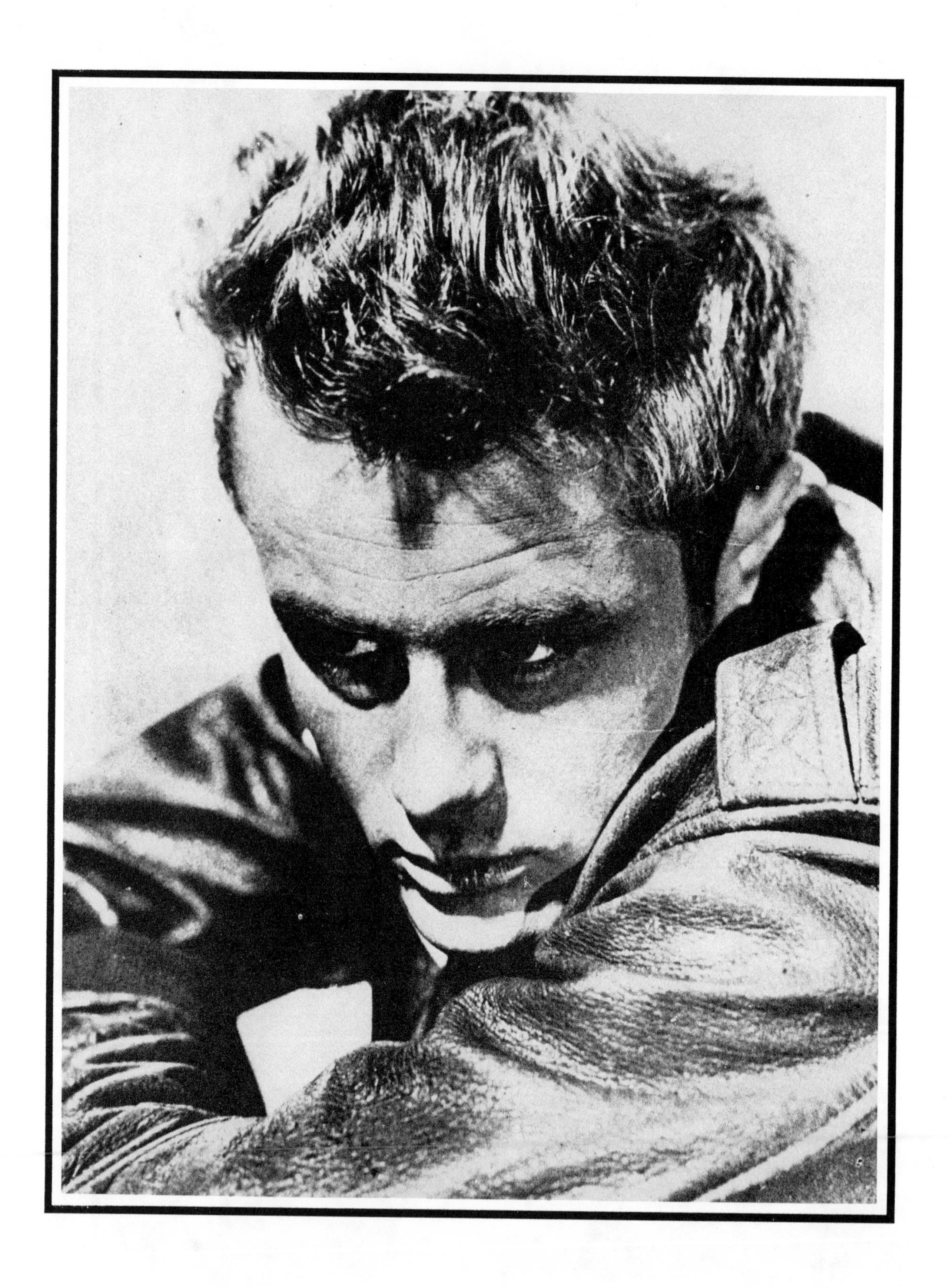

In James Dean
day's youth discover
self. Less for the
easons usually
dvanced—violence,
adism, hysteria,
essimism, cruelty and
lth—than for others
finitely more simple
nd commonplace;
nodesty of feeling;
ontinual fantasy life;
noral purity, without
elation to everyday
norality but all the
nore rigorous; eternal
dolescent love of tests
nd trials;
ntoxication, pride, and
egret at feeling
neself 'outside'
ociety; refusal and
lesire to become
ntegrated; and finally
icceptance, or refusal,
of the world as it is."
— Francois Truffaut,
Arts, 1956

PART THREE

James Dean: The Legend

JAMES DEAN
MOVIE ACTOR
1931 1955
A LEGEND IN HIS
LIFETIME
MARION QUARTERBACK CLUB

James Dean: The Legend

"America has known many rebellions— but, never one like this: millions of teenage rebels heading for nowhere, some in 'hot-rod' cars, others on the blare of rock n' roll music, some with guns in their hands. And at their head—a dead leader."
—Picture Post, October 8, 1956

Does a James Dean legend truly exist? If so, what and who created it? How does such a legend develop? And why did a legend form around James Dean?

The first two sections of DEANMANIA sought to define THE MAN and THE CHARACTER of James Dean on the pretext that without them, the establishment of the third dimension, James Dean THE LEGEND would, at best, be shallow and superficial. It seems safe at this point to admit that while the two previous dimensions provided the physical substance necessary for the creation of a legend, it is equally clear The Legend rests completely in the minds and hands of his devoted fans. They have celebrated his very existence now for better than thirty-five years. Without devoted family, friends, and fans the very elements that are James Dean the Person and the Character would be just elements—it is the magic created by this group that gathers around the memory that transcends and creates the dimension of The Legend.

David Dalton, in JAMES DEAN AMERICAN ICON, prefers to use the word "cult" rather than "legend", when detailing what has happened since James Dean died in 1955: "[w]hile fan clubs form around living stars, cults form around the dead or divinized. A cult, even of a popular culture hero, could not exist without its sacrificial victim."

It is evident that in James Dean we have the sacrificial figure that Dalton concludes is "the necessary link between the mundane and the sacred...." To assign cultic status to all that has happened since that ill-fated evening in September 1955 seems unrealistic. Too often today negative connotations are associated with the cultic. Too many positive manifestations associate with James Dean and his following today to assign it anything but legendary status. These manifestations are the very topics discussed in this final section of DEANMANIA.

Fan clubs play a major role in perpetuating the memory and spirit of James Dean. Such clubs form around deceased as well as living stars. The activities shared by members of the James Dean fan clubs demonstrate that they more frequently celebrate beliefs and notions they hold about James Dean than dwell on the fact that he is dead. The majority of Dean fans continue to celebrate what he was; it is only the rare few, who have become obsessed with his death, that approach anything cultic in nature.

Immediately after his death, such headlines appeared as "Did Jimmy Dean Really Die?"; "James Dean is not Dead!"; and "Jimmy Dean Returns!—Read His Own Words from the Beyond." Fortunately for James Dean and his fans, persons typically raising such questions seldom dedicate themselves to learning what is true and what is not. This is to say, most of these people simply are only interested in items which support their continuing delusions about James Dean.

What follows is a wealth of information about the many visible and tangible means that have helped to create the legend associated with James Dean. Included are the many sites important during James Dean's early life in Fairmount Indiana as well as the memorials that have appeared since his death. These are clearly manifestations of the extent to which family, friends and fans are willing to go in order to be certain that his memory remains visible for generations to come.

Also included is a look at the hundreds of collectible items that have appeared since Dean's death ranging from the most mundane to the rarest of James Dean memorabilia. Several Dean fans have written short notes about their collections to share with readers and these are included along with the highlight of this section, extensive material from a single collection belonging to Enrico Perego of Milano, Italy.

James Dean fans are dedicated to perpetuating his memory and spirit. This dedication is manifested in the many ways featured in this section. For the last 35 years, James Dean's fans have continued to provide new generations with an enlightened understanding of James Dean THE LEGEND.

The town which helped form James Dean.

photo by Denny Hill

ON THIS SITE STOOD THE SEVEN GABLES
WHERE JAMES DEAN
ONE OF THE MOST CHARISMATIC
AND IDOLIZED MOVIE ACTORS
OF ALL TIME WAS BORN...
FEBRUARY 8, 1931.
ERECTED BY
MARION QUARTERBACK CLUB

Marion, Indiana

photo by Denny Hill

James Dean's Birthplace

Ten miles north of Fairmount, Indiana lies Marion, Indiana. Here in 1931 James Byron Dean was born to Winton and Mildred (Wilson) Dean. Jim spent his first four years at the Green Gables Apartments and then in 1935 he and his parents moved to Santa Monica, California where he would remain until his mother's death from cancer in 1940. After his mother's death his father decided that it would be best for Jim to return to Fairmount, Indiana where he would be raised by his Uncle Marcus and Aunt Ortense Winslow. So he boarded the train with his grandmother Emma Dean and began his journey to Fairmount, where he spent the next nine years of his life.

Although the Green Gables Apartments are no longer standing, the Marion Quarterback Club placed two plaques on the site of the former apartment building to serve as a reminder to visitors that this was the place where James Dean was born.

Fairmount, Indiana

photo by Denny Hill

James Dean's Hometown

WELCOME to Fairmount, Indiana!

Population 3,286.

Hometown of James Byron Dean, "Garfield" Jim Davis and Phil Jones. The culture center of Indiana. A city which has 14 times the national average of persons listed in "Who's Who of America." From this small town have come college presidents, artists, authors, scientists, inventors, the founder of the State of Oklahoma, and an actor—JAMES BYRON DEAN.

The people in Fairmount are warm, friendly and very accommodating, yet you can't help but notice a reluctance to volunteer more information than necessary when it comes to talking about James Dean. Most will discuss Jim freely to a point, but it seems important to realize that life in Fairmount must go on in spite of the notoriety James Dean has brought this small Midwestern town. The presence of James Dean has not been forgotten, but unlike many towns which find themselves in similar positions, Fairmount has remained just another friendly small town in the Midwest.

The first-time visitor to Fairmount finds many sites important in the life of James Dean. Each deserves a visit. However, it seems important to stress that the places a fan might visit in Fairmount, while important to the life of James Dean, are today (in most cases) not public attractions, and thus when visiting Fairmount, one should approach many of the Dean sites with respect. After all, you will be visiting his boyhood home (now the home of his cousin, Marcus Winslow Jr. and his family); the church where he attended services and where in October 1955 his funeral was held; a motorcycle shop where he played (now private property); Park Cemetery (where Dean and family members are buried); downtown Fairmount (where he spent time as a young man with his friends); and Fairmount High School (today in danger of being demolished).

In addition to these places, a visit to Fairmount should include time spent at the Fairmount Historical Museum (which houses the most authentic collection of James Dean memorabilia) and the James Dean Gallery (the largest private collection of Dean memorabilia on public display). Both collections present fans and visitors alike with excellent displays of items that bear the image of James Dean and have been instrumental in the establishment of James Dean The Legend.

photo by Denny Hill

The Winslow Family Home: Jim's Boyhood Home

James Dean came to live here in 1940 after his mother died. His father, unable to care for him as a young boy, agreed that it would be best for Jim to return to Indiana where he would be raised by Mr. and Mrs. Marcus Winslow. The Winslow family home, originally built for Ansel and Ida Winslow in 1904, became Jim's home after his return from California. This fourteen room house, today well cared for and maintained by Jim's cousin, Marcus Winslow Jr., overlooks more than 250 acres.

It was here that Jim learned a great deal about farming. In an interview with famed Hollywood columnist Hedda Hopper, Jim once remarked that "getting healthy can be hazardous, this was a real farm that I was on and I worked like crazy—as long as someone was watching me. The forty acres of oats was a huge stage and when the audience left I took a nap and things didn't get plowed or harrowed."

Fairmount High School

(compiled from notes by Anne Warr, Fairmount Town Historian, 1988)

Fairmount High School received its commission in 1898. It was completed in 1902 with three additions added at later dates. The first class to graduate from it was the class of 1900. Jim attended high school here and graduated with the class of 1949. Under Jim's picture, the yearbook bears the inscription, "Jim is our regular basketball guy, and when you're around him time will fly."

It was at Fairmount High School that Jim would become acquainted with Mrs. Adeline (Brookshire) Nall, 110his speech teacher and first drama coach. Her influence would be felt for many years to come.

Fairmount High School became a middle school in 1970 and was officially closed on May 30, 1986.

Today the fate of the school building has yet to be determined. However, many Dean fans, as well as several citizens of Fairmount, clearly want to see the building remain. On Saturday May 27, 1989 The Madison-Grant Youth Sports Center and Magic City Street Rods, Inc. held a benefit "Cruise-In and Sock Hop" with all proceeds to be used for building upkeep. As recently as May 1990 it was obvious that the fate of this Dean landmark remained undecided. While a decision awaits, the building continues to deteriorate rapidly.

photo by Denny Hill

LEFT: Fairmount High School Graduating Class of 1949 JAMES DEAN, fifth row, fourth from the left ROBERT PULLEY, sixth row, third from the left (upper left-hand corner)

BELOW: James Dean, brilliant senior guard, was one of the main cogs in the Quaker line-up this season. Jim was rated as one of the most outstanding guards in the county. (1949 Fairmount High School Yearbook.

courtesy Fairmount Historical Museum

Back Creek Friend's Church

As a boy Jim attended Sunday meetings in the Back Creek Friends Church. This Quaker church while unadorned outside boasts a mural of Christ as the Good Shepherd inside. On October 8, 1955, James Dean's funeral services were conducted here. An annual memorial service is now held each September 30, at 1 PM, concluding with a walk to Park Cemetery.

Carter's Cycle Shop

Just two doors down from the Winslow farm was Marvin Carter's cycle shop. Jim, like many young boys in Fairmount, had a motorcycle (he got his first in 1947, a Czech model), and he and the other boys would tinker with their cycles at Carter's shop. Frequently, Jim would line up races and use the loudspeaker system at Carter's to announce the race. Local boys recall at different times how very authentic Dean made the announcement of each race sound.

Park Cemetery

Near the Winslow family home, The Back Creek Friends Church, and Carter's Cycle Shop, north of town, on the left-hand side of the road, along what was Main Street while driving through Fairmount, lies Park Cemetery. Here, surrounded by the spots most important to Jim during his life in Fairmount, he was buried amidst several other Deans and Winslows.

It is rare to visit the grave when there are no fresh flowers. Fans still continue to visit Dean's grave on an almost daily basis, and they frequently leave flowers, letters, and other items of special significance. Each is left because it enables the one leaving it to express the sentiments he/she needs to convey.

In addition to the headstone that marks the site of Dean's grave, there is another monument which was established in 1957, a brick pillar with a bust of Dean on top and a plaque and JAMES DEAN inscribed on the front. Unfortunately, it too has met the fate of Dean's original headstone. Both the headstone and the bust and plaque disappeared soon after they were put in place. The headstone seems to have reappeared some eight years later, but the original stone was so badly defaced, visitors to the grave today find a replacement marker, which simply reads:

JAMES B. DEAN

1931-1955

The monument originally held a bust of James Dean on top and remains but a reminder to visitors who pass by it on their way to Dean's grave. Atop the brick pillar visitors find the metal rod that once supported the bust of Dean. Below, the front of the pillar bears the words: JAMES DEAN. Part of the 'E' in Dean is missing and below these two words there is an empty spot which originally contained a plaque. This brick pillar is set upon a circular brick foundation with a mosaic pattern at its base. Slowly, but surely, visitors have begun to pick away the tiny pieces of mosaic pattern.

While visiting with Bob Pulley, he indicated that presently there is talk about placing another bust atop this monument. It is hoped that now, out of respect for James Dean, it might remain for all to see and to appreciate.

ABOVE PICTURED: the monument as it appears today, 1990 close-up of name on brick pillar monument, and headstone marker for Dean

Fairmount Historical Museum

The dedication ceremony for the Fairmount Historical Museum was held September 21, 1975, with about 2,000 people in attendance. The first temporary location of the museum was over the Western Auto Store on South Main Street. Eight years later the museum was moved to its permanent home at the Dr. J. W. Patterson house and office at 209 E. Washington Street.

Today the museum is open daily, May through October from 1 PM to 4 PM, seven days a week and other times by appointment. Once each year the Museum Board sponsors the annual Fairmount "Museum Days" festival which began in 1975. This three day event, always held the last weekend in September, pays special recognition to Fairmount natives who have made a distinct mark in the world. In the past 15 years "Museum Days" attendance has gradually grown to over 20,000 people annually.

Dean fans will find a very interesting collection of Dean memorabilia at the museum. Here fans can view the most authentic collection of Dean collectibles. Included among the items are many personal belonging: one of his cycles; boots worn in GIANT; numerous awards and racing trophies; all of which have been donated or loaned to the museum by immediate family members. Original sketches done by Dean himself while in grade school are also on display. The collection also includes several rare magazines and books as well as numerous other interesting items of memorabilia.

The next few pages exhibit photographs of some of the memorabilia on display at the museum. The museum also includes a gift shop where fans/visitors can buy James Dean collectibles.

All photography accompanying this section Courtesy Fairmount Historical Museum/ Photography by Denny Hill)

No visitor (especially a Dean fan) should miss an opportunity to browse the collection at the Fairmount Historical Museum. You might even be lucky enough to visit on a day when Bob Pulley, President of the Fairmount Historical Society and one of Dean's hometown friends, is working. If Bob's not working, there are other citizens from Fairmount who donate their time to the museum, and they too are helpful and delightful to visit with about James Dean.

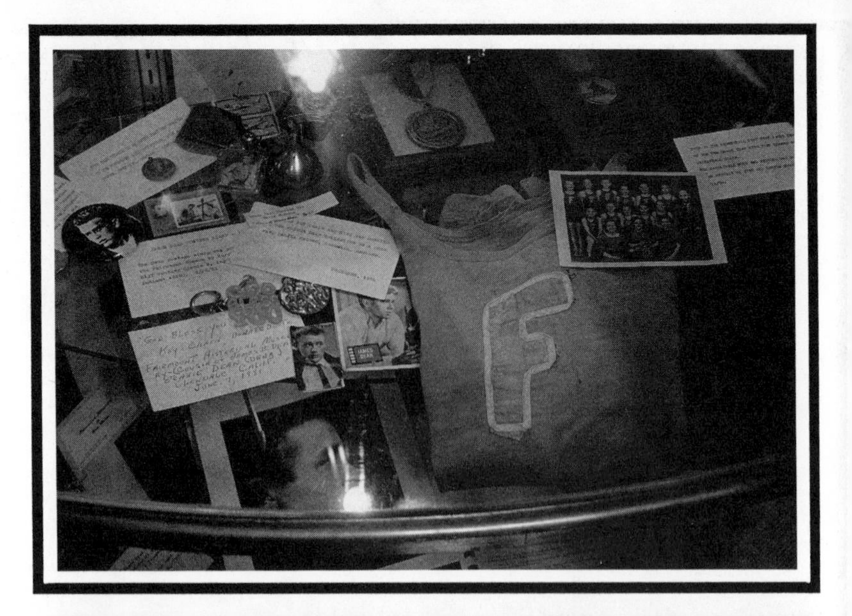

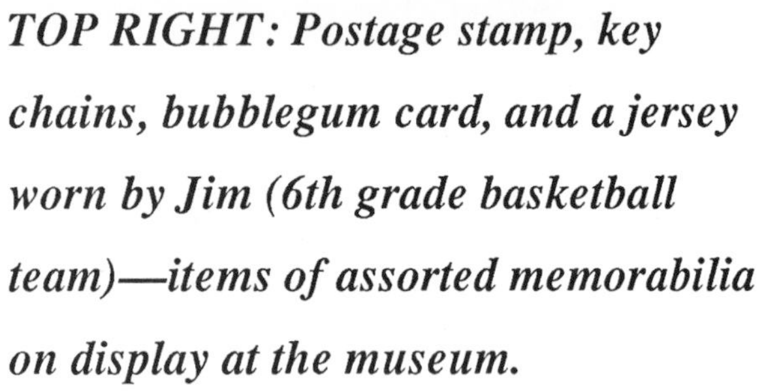

TOP RIGHT: Postage stamp, key chains, bubblegum card, and a jersey worn by Jim (6th grade basketball team)—items of assorted memorabilia on display at the museum.
LOWER RIGHT: Awards, mostly given posthumously, loaned to the museum by Winton Dean, James Dean's father.

TOP LEFT: This clay bust was one Dean himself was sculpting when he was killed. To preserve it, it has been cast in permastone.

LOWER LEFT: Dean's bongos; letter sweaters; bust which was displayed at Fairmount High School; and an original model of the monument placed at Park Cemetery in 1957.

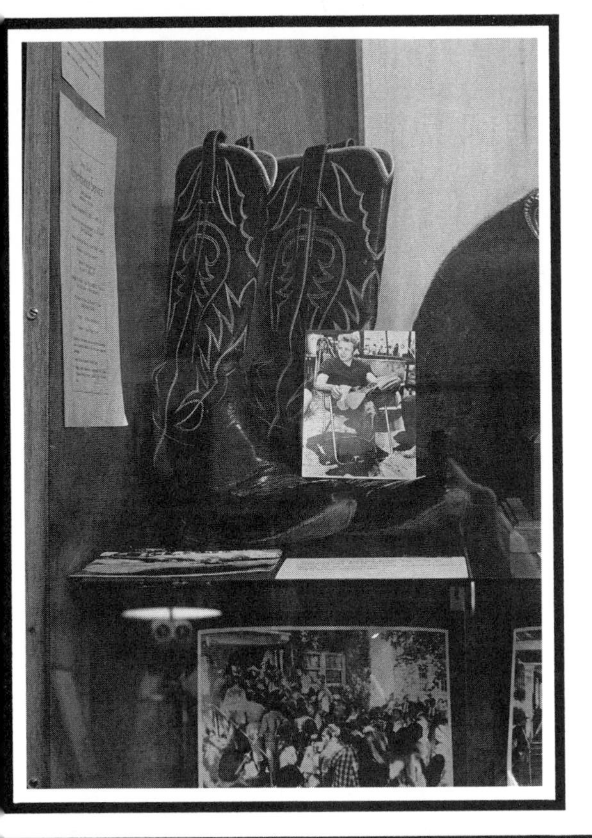

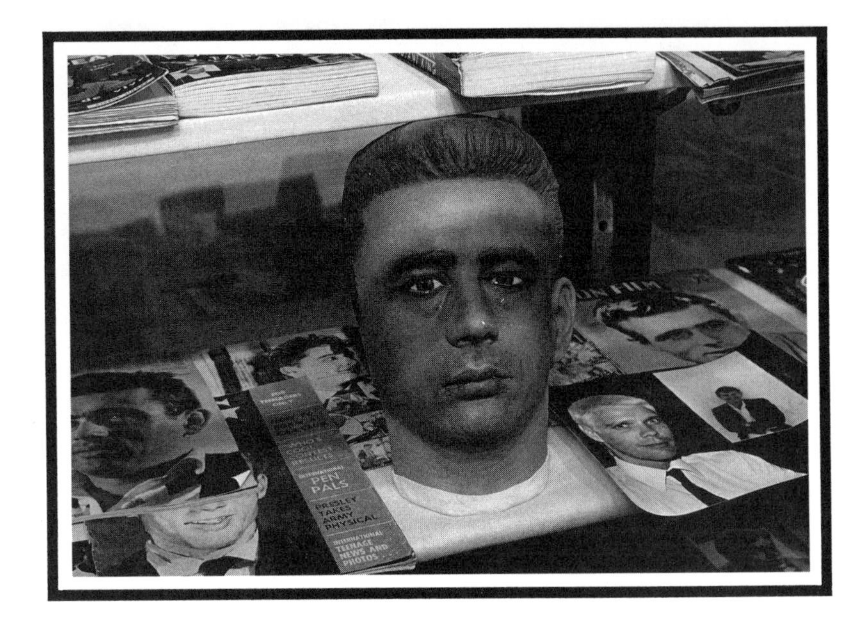

TOP LEFT: Boots worn by Dean on the set of GIANT, magazines and books on display.

TOP RIGHT: Rare Dean life-mask donated to the museum by Brian O'Dowd. This mask originally had a cigarette dangling in Dean fashion—it was removed at the request of relatives.

LEFT: Books and magazines on display.

TOP LEFT: David Mannweiler in the INDIANAPOLIS NEWS, April 10, 1989, wrote an interesting article about the discovery of Dean's motorcycle. It seems that since the bike was never registered under James Dean's name (it was registered under the name of the shop that sold the bike), the person who eventually had possession of it didn't realize what he had. Marcus Winslow Jr., at the request of Dean fans, hired a retired Indianapolis police lieutenant to investigate the whereabouts of this cycle. It was located, restored, and is now displayed at the museum.

BELOW AND LEFT: Memorabilia for sale in the gift shop at the museum. Visitors and fans can select from books, magazines, posters, cups, shirts, postcards, plates, license plates, paper weights, and a variety of other collectible items—each bearing witness to the fact that James Dean remains very popular and marketable today.

BOTTOM LEFT: More books and magazines.

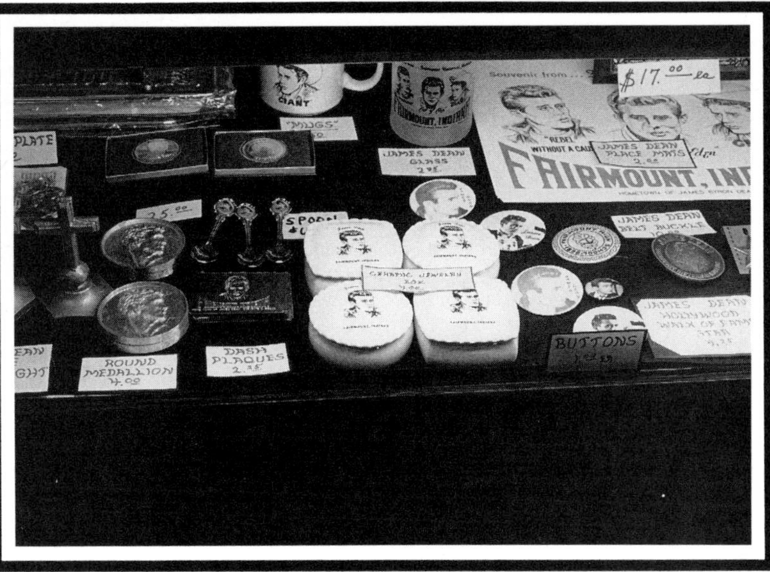

Magazines and memorabilia of James Dean housed at the Fairmount Historical Museum.

FAIRMOUNT "MUSEUM DAYS" - SEPTEMBER 22-23-24, 1989

The Fairmount Historical Museum Officers and Directors, sponsors of the 14th annual "Museum Days/Remembering James Dean", and the Town of Fairmount extend a HEARTY WELCOME to visitors and friends from several parts of the world who have traveled here to attend our September Festival.

The Fairmount Museum/Authentic James Dean Exhibit, can be viewed daily at 203 E. Washington St., one block E. of the traffic light in downtown Fairmount. The home that houses the Museum is on the National Register of Historic places and is a must to tour. The Museum has a Gift Shop.

****

FRIDAY - JIMMIE CHANOS CARNIVAL - MAIN STREET, AND LIVE ENTERTAINMENT (3 days)
12 PM - Streets closed off. Activities in full swing by 5:30 PM.
4 PM - Dean Film - "Rebel Without A Cause" - Municipal Building, 214 West Washington Street.
5 PM - RAYZ OF SUNSHINE AND BAND, Entertainment Stage (Main Street)
5-9 PM -Eastern Star, Chicken & Noodle meals; Saturday 11 AM - ?
10 AM-- 9 PM - Registration - 50's, Classic & Antique Car Show at Playacres Park (Cruise-In) Magic City Street Rods, Hosts.

FRIDAY - SAT. - SUN. - MUSEUM INFORMATION BOOTH, in front of Ben Franklin.

SATURDAY - Festivities will start at 8:30 AM
9 AM - 5th annual James Dean Memorial 10-K Run - Citizens Tele. Co.
10 AM - Childrens Pet Parade, Start at Mill & 2nd Sts., 9:45 AM.
8 AM - 1 PM - Fussgangers Volksmarch (10-K Walk) Corner-Tyler & Syc.
11 AM - KIDDIE TRACTOR PULL, (3) Weight Classes - up to 45 Lbs.; 46-55 lbs.; 56-65 lbs. Held in front of Library.
12 NOON - JAMES DEAN ROCK LASSO CONTEST * Entertainment Stage.
1:00 PM - Special Recognition Ceremony at Entertainment Stage.
2 PM - GRAND PARADE - starts at Tyler & Sycamore Streets & passes down S. Main St., to Madison, West on Madison to Mill St., North on Mill St., to Washington,St., E. on Washington & ends at Elm St. Check at Information Booth FOR PARADE WINNERS - 4 PM.
3:15 PM - TWIN CITY CLOGGERS & SQUARE DANCE - Main Street.
4 PM - James Dean Film - "GIANT" - Municipal Building.
5 PM - PLAYHOUSE DANCE STUDIO, Marion, IN, Main Street Stage.
6 PM - CHARLIE CROPPER - WWKI RADIO, Kokomo, IN.
7 PM - "GARFIELD" Cat Photo Contest Winners announced, on Stage.
8:30 PM - BEST 50's DANCE CONTEST, with Cropper, Main Street.
9:00 PM - JAMES DEAN LOOK-A-LIKE CONTEST, Main Street Stage.
Tours - Old Fairmount High School by Madison-Grant Youth Basketball League. Admission charge.

FRIDAY - SAT. - SUN. - Tour the Fairmount Museum, Go to Playacres Park to see the James Dean Memorial Rod Show. Museum open Sept. 30th.

SUNDAY - 9:30 AM - Attend Church Services at the Church of your choice.
12 NOON - JAMES DEAN BICYCLE TOUR - Start at Museum lawn.
1:00 PM - CHORDS CARE AND REPAIR BARBERSHOP QUARTET.
1:30 PM - GOSPEL SINGERS - Spencer & Sharon Bunch, Lori Baxter, Miriam Rich and the Baptist Church Trio.
2:15 PM - MADISON-GRANT HIGH SCHOOL BAND CONCERT. MUSEUM LAWN.
2:45 PM - MADISON-GRANT HIGH SCHOOL Ar-Guys 'n Gals. Main Street.
3:30 PM - SOUNDS OF FRIENDSHIP CHOIR. Main Street Stage.
4:15 PM - Nolder Underwood (Senior Citizen) Favorite Hymn.
4:30 PM - DJ SPECIAL - Phillip L. Ruley, The Ruler of Rock & Roll
3:00 PM - James Dean Film - "EAST OF EDEN" - Municipal Building.

****Bring Your Lawn Chair For All Programs****

SEPTEMBER 30th - 1:30 PM - James Dean Memorial Service, Back Creek Friends Ch.

Fairmount Museum Days

Each year thousands of people come to Fairmount the last weekend in September. They come from all over the United States, Canada, and indeed many come from all parts of the world. Each of them comes in order to participate in three days of celebration to honor Fairmount notables, in particular, one well-known son, JAMES DEAN.

Imagine spending three days surrounded by thousands of James Dean fans. Events during this celebration include a James Dean Memorial Rod Run; Classic/Antique car show; James Dean Rock Lasso contest; parades; bicycle tours; Dean Look-A-Like contest; best 50s dress and dance; live entertainment—continually playing 50s music. In addition to these activities, visitors can see all of Dean's movies as well as rare television appearances.

This three-day celebration truly demonstrates how widespread Dean's popularity has become. It is difficult to explain the sentiments and emotions that this celebration creates in Dean's fans. The festival is however a true manifestation of the creation of JAMES DEAN THE LEGEND.

Fairmount Historical Museum, Inc.

1990  1990

203 East Washington Street
P.O. Box 92
Fairmount, Indiana 46928

Museum Tours
Authentic James Dean Exhibit

James Byron Dean, idolized movie star, born February 8, 1931, Marion, Indiana. Graduate of Fairmount High School, outstanding athlete, thespian. Attended Back Creek Quaker Meetings. Dean starred in East of Eden, Rebel Without a Cause and Giant - all made in the same year. Instant success. Dean died September 30, 1955 (head-on automobile accident in California). Buried in Park Cemetery, Fairmount, Indiana. Dean still lives in the hearts of many people.
Fairmount Historical Museum, Inc.
Fairmount, Indiana 46928

FAIRMOUNT MUSEUM DAYS

FRIDAY
SATURDAY & SUNDAY

SEPTEMBER 28th, 29th, 30th
FAIRMOUNT, INDIANA
Grand Parade - Saturday, 2:00 P.M.

For further information phone:
(317) 948-4555 (museum)
or
(317) 948-4444 or (317) 948-5382

Museum Hours: May through October
1:00 P.M. - 4:00 P.M. Daily or by Appointment

N MAIN ST.
OURTH ST.
The James Dean Gallery
Dean Gallery

The James Dean Gallery

On Thursday, September 22nd, 1989 in Fairmount Indiana, THE JAMES DEAN GALLERY, which houses the world's largest private collection of James Dean memorabilia, opened for public display. The exhibit, the private collection of David Loehr, Dean archivist, includes thousands of items including clothing from his films, high school yearbooks, a rare Warner Brothers life-mask, and hundreds of original movie posters, books, and magazines from over twenty different countries from around the world. Also included are hundreds of tribute and novelty items that have been produced since the 1950s, such as plates, mugs, busts, puzzles, and gum cards.

The Gallery provides fans with an opportunity to view many of the items which have contributed to keeping the memory of James Dean alive. The gallery is open daily from 10:00 am until 5:00 pm. Admission is $2.00. A new feature will be a private screening room in which Dean movies and rare footage of Dean television appearances will be shown.

"Fairmount is great! And David's James Dean Gallery is really something to see."
—Betty Couyou, Massachusetts

"With Adeline Nall at my side I was relieved to turn the mike over to her as quickly as possible! She grabbed everyone's attention and gave a touching, relevant speech. Then she read to me a beautiful telegram of congratulations sent by Sylvia. The highlight was when Adeline dramatically snapped open a switch-blade knife which was supplied by Kenneth Kendall, to cut the ribbon and officially open 'The James Dean Gallery'"

—David Loehr, Gallery Owner

(remarks at opening ceremonies)

"...Our first stop was David's 'James Dean Gallery'. The clothing of Jimmy's and everything in the Gallery was wonderful. David has given so much of his time and energy to make this gallery a monument to James Dean's memory...."
—Karen LeDuc, Canada

David Loehr recalls for us how he first became interested in James Dean, and how the The Gallery came to be established:

"My interest in James Dean first started in 1974 when my friend Bob Rodriguez gave me a hardbound copy of JAMES DEAN THE MUTANT KING by David Dalton. Inside the book Bob inscribed, 'There's a lot in here about us...You!' Until that time I only knew the name James Dean, and nothing else about him. I was never much of a reader, but I found myself intrigued with the story and read it straight through.

"The following spring I saw EAST OF EDEN for the first time at the Los Angeles Film Exposition on a big screen in Cinemascope. I was knocked out by Dean's performance. Later that year I saw EDEN, REBEL, GIANT and Robert Altman's 1957 documentary THE JAMES DEAN STORY at a three week 'Rebel Series' which featured James Dean, Montgomery Clift, and John Garfield at the Los Angeles County Art Museum. I was fortunate to see all three of Dean's films on a big screen for the first time.

"I began searching memorabilia shops, bookstores and flea markets for anything concerning James Dean. I found photos, books, magazines, and posters. Items seemed scarce since Dean had been gone 20 years. Gradually I found things, and before long my collection filled an entire cardboard box!

"In May of 1979 (on Mother's Day) while driving from Los Angeles to New York, I made my first visit to Fairmount. I visited The Fairmount Historical Museum which at that time was located above the Auto Parts store on Main Street. I was greeted by Mattie Brown and Jimmy's High School Speech and Drama teacher, Adeline Nall. I was impressed with the small hometown exhibit of James Dean memorabilia and actual artifacts.

"From there I visited Dean's grave site and stopped at the Winslow farm where Dean was raised. Aunt Ortense invited me in, and I could hardly believe I was there. That whole first visit in Fairmount lasted only three hours.

"The rest of the trip to New York, my head was buzzing with ideas about the town and museum. I couldn't wait to go back. For the next several years, I visited the town and did whatever I could to help support the Historical Museum.

"As the years passed my collection grew to the point where I realized it should be put on public display somewhere. In August of 1987 I purchased the beautiful 12 room house at 425 N. Main Street in Fairmount, and on September 22, 1988 The James Dean Gallery opened to the public. For the opening ceremonies the local high school band played and Adeline Nall cut the ribbon with a switchblade knife lent her by Kenneth Kendall."

Loehr's collection on display at the "James Dean Gallery" includes the following items, most of which are original, dating from 1942 to the present and drawn from over 20 countries around the world:

* over 80 magazines with Dean featured on the cover

* over 140 books, both hardback and and paperback relating to Dean (fiction and non-fiction)

* several dozen original movie posters and lobby cards

* soundtrack and tribute record albums, singles, and sheet music

* copies of Fairmount High School yearbooks, from 1945 through 1949, each featuring Dean as a student

* an outfit (shirt, pants and belt) worn by Dean in EAST OF EDEN

* the brown wool trousers worn by Dean in the famous knife fight scene in REBEL WITHOUT A CAUSE

* a basketball jersey worn by Jimmy in 1942

* autographs obtained by fans in 1955

* a copy of the rare life-mask made by the Warner Brothers make-up department during the production of GIANT

* the original wax head of James Dean that was on display for over 20 years at The Coney Island Wax Museum

* over 1,000 photographs, including many never published shots

* memorial and tribute items including rare scarves, plates, busts and medallions from the 1950s and other more recent items such as cups, metal boxes, pencil sharpeners, and stationary

* numerous rare and unusual items that have been produced since the 1950s

To see everything the first time is impossible. Fortunately, Mary Ann Michna and Pam Schwetz, members of "We Remember Dean International", have recently made available, The James Dean Gallery Video Postcard, a 10-minute video tour of the Gallery. The tape includes an introduction by David Loehr, owner and Dean archivist, and music by Jeff and Kris Miller of Fairmount, Indiana. This videotape is available at the James Dean Gallery.

JAMES DEAN
1931Feb8 – 1955Sep30pm5:59

James Dean Memorial

Highway 46, Cholame, California

"Death is the one Inevitable, Undeniable truth. In it lies the only ultimate nobility for man. Beyond it, through immortality, the only hope."
—James Dean

It was at the intersection of Highways 46 and 41, near Cholame California, that James Dean met with his tragic death, September 30, 1955 at 5:59 p.m. Warren Newton Beath writes in "The Death of James Dean" that "Near the highway is a tree. Snaked around it is a gleaming chromium sculpture as striking and anomalous as a spaceship settled in the desert in a 1950s horror movie. It was built and brought here from Japan in 1977 by a rich Japanese businessman named Seita Ohnishi at a cost of $15,000."

The memorial reads quite simply:

JAMES DEAN

1931 Feb 8 — 1955 Sep 30 pm 5:59

Following the 5:59 is the symbol of infinity. How fitting a tribute to James Dean. This site has become important in recent years because of the James Dean Memorial Car Rally, founded by Roger Cannon of Carmel California. Each year Dean fans return to the scene in order to retrace the steps their hero took from Los Angeles that fateful day in September 1955.

On the occasion of the twenty-sixth anniversary of Dean's death, Seita Ohnishi returned to the memorial, established by him four years earlier. Through an interpreter, Mr. Onishi reminded Dean fans that day at the memorial that Dean's "...fame is international; his impact, historic. He was the brief, living manifestation of a new era, the persona to which a whole generation pinned its hopes for a better tomorrow. He was more than merely a movie star. He was, and remains, a symbol....

"Yet this monument is not intended to be merely a tribute to James Dean. It is also meant to be a reaffirmation of the value of all human life. That is why, in accordance with an old Japanese custom, this marker has been placed at the site of the accident that took his life, to serve both as a memorial to the young man I so admired and a reminder to all that life is a precious gift to be preserved at all costs...."

Jerry Emory, writing in IMAGE (March 1988) describes the monument as "eerily impressive, [and it] is worth seeing any time of the year—and in some ways it's at its best when it's most deserted. Whether or not you consider yourself a James Dean admirer, you are likely to find the drive into California's empty quarter an inspiring expedition through wide-open country that stirs the soul. The visit amplifies the memorial's parting reflection on James Dean: 'Death in youth is life that glows eternal.'"

9-30-55

We started out that autumn day
With thoughts of happiness
But we did not know what lied ahead
Our fate we could not guess

What went wrong, we'll never know
Our fault we could not see
But our life was taken, forever gone,
The waste of all to be.

I did not think of death that day
But it had thought of me
Our car held but the two of us
And IMMORTALITY.

—Ken Grant, Missouri

Griffith Observatory Monument

"Mozart may have written his own requiem, but James Dean ordered his own monument."
— Kenneth Kendall

On Tuesday November 1, 1988, Friends of the Observatory, a non-profit community support group dedicated to the development of Griffith Observatory, held a ceremony to unveil and dedicate a bronze bust of James Dean, that was donated to the city of Los Angeles and Griffith Observatory by artist, Kenneth Kendall. In 1955 at Dean's request, Kenneth Kendall met and began to sculpt Dean's image.

James Dean's association with Griffith Observatory began in 1955 when the filming of REBEL WITHOUT A CAUSE took place in the planetarium. This association continues to be important to visitors who repeatedly inquire about the locations used in REBEL.

Sylvia Bongiovanni, Editor of the "We Remember Dean International" newsletter recalls the event:

"The day had arrived. After three years of planning, Kenneth's day was finally here. The official ceremonies at Griffith began at 10:00 am and drew a number of people, about 100 or so! Ms. Kara Knack of the Friends of the Observatory (who organized the day's events) opened the dedication services by introducing Dr. E. C. Krupp, director of Griffith Observatory. He spoke of the Observatory's role in REBEL WITHOUT A CAUSE, mentioning that the film was the first in which the Observatory was portrayed for what it is...Four REBEL gang members were there: Frank Mazzola, Jack Grinnage, Beverly Long, and Steffi Sidney, as was Faye Mayo, Natalie's stand-in for REBEL...Another Dean friend present was Ms. Maila Nurmi! She was delightful, telling stories galore about Jimmy. Ms. Knack then introduced Mr. Kenneth Kendall and he spoke of his work on the bust, how it all began shortly after Jimmy died, and how it came to be on display at Griffith...Kenneth was an inspiration to us all that day—it was very exciting and touching to say the least...The monument stands to the right of the observatory as you approach it and is really something to see! One of the finest, if not the finest, artworks of James Dean, it is indeed the everlasting tribute to Jimmy. A visit to Griffith Observatory is now a definite must for all James Dean fans!!! To see Jimmy in this place of honor is something you'll remember for a very long time to come."

The plaque below the star on front of the monument reads as follows:

"Key scenes from the classic REBEL WITHOUT A CAUSE were filmed at Griffith Observatory in Spring 1955. Although many movies have been filmed at Griffith Observatory, REBEL WITHOUT A CAUSE was the first to portray the observatory as what it is and to contribute positively to the observatory's international reputation. The monument acknowledges Griffith Observatory's long and continuous involvement with Hollywood film production by remembering the young star of that motion picture.

Creator of the bust, artist Kenneth Kendall and "WRDI" Club co-founder Sylvia Bongiovanni on dedication day.

photo courtesy Sylvia Bongiovanni

A plaque on the back of the monument reads as follows:

1931 JAMES DEAN 1955

This is not a monument to a Rebel. Those were only roles he played. James Dean was an American original who on a basis of high school honors and in a period of five years rose to the very pinnacle of the theatrical profession and through the magic of motion pictures lives on in legend.

Presented in 1988 by the Artist Kenneth Kendall who sculpted it in 1955-1956 at the request of James Dean and dedicates it to his memory."

It ended with his body changed to light
A star that burns forever in that sky

—"The Flight of Quetzalcoatl"

Artist Kenneth Kendall and the bust at Griffith Park.

photo courtesy of Sylvia Bongiovanni

Collecting James Dean

(Portions of this section have appeared earlier in articles about James Dean collectibles written by the author)

Perhaps James Dean himself said it best when he told his friend Dr. James DeWeerd, "if a man can bridge the gap between life and death. I mean if he can live on after he's dead, then maybe he was a great man...to me the only success, the only greatness, is immortality."

Few would argue that James Dean has not reached this plateau of greatness. To many fans he is immortal—still today, thirty-five years after his death, his movies continue to be watched and enjoyed, and the world of James Dean collectibles grows larger and larger with each passing day. To some, Dean epitomized the 1950s youth rebellion. The 1950s youth immediately saw in him a reflection of themselves—never before had a single individual so clearly and so dramatically portrayed teenage frustrations.

It is obvious that in 1955 few people realized the impact James Dean would have on American Culture. However, the years immediately following his tragic death saw the development of a following that continues to grow today and appears to become stronger as time passes. Today's appreciation of James Dean seems to be predicated on his truly remarkable ability to portray whatever emotions and reactions were required of him in his roles as Cal Trask, Jim Stark, and Jett Rink. Compare this to earlier "scream and shout" appreciation demonstrated by hundreds of 1950s youth immediately following his death and you have two distinctly differing periods of adulation—each unique to a period and each founded on differing perceptions of James Dean. Yet, what is remarkable about both is that in many ways they compliment each other.

James Dean is still today growing in popularity and appreciation. This is best demonstrated by the extent to which Dean memorabilia has both increased in value and in number of items to collect.

Today the fantastic array of James Dean memorabilia produced to honor or memorialize this incredibly popular film star provides the true "Dean-o-phile" with a challenge to see what items, most of which were issued posthumously, he/she can add to a seemingly limitless collection.

Would-be collectors expect to find items such as photographs (movie stills), posters (including original movie release posters), postcards, stamps, decals, bubblegum cards, coffee mugs, glasses, plates, cigarette lighters, buttons, pins, sew-ons, sweatshirts, t-shirts and so forth. While it is important not to lessen the collectibility of these items, it is nevertheless the intent of this section to focus more specifically on books, magazines, movie related items and many of the truly rare Dean collectibles.

As has been the case with many famous people—Marilyn Monroe, Elvis Presley, Judy Garland, and countless others, their deaths provide many with an opportunity to exploit and cash in on their often shortened lives. This was the case with James Dean. It was only a short time after his death that newsstands were covered with magazines wholly devoted to his life and career. These so-called tribute magazines were mass produced in 1956, with the total number published approaching two million copies. Included here are JIMMY DEAN RETURNS, THE JAMES DEAN ALBUM, THE REAL JAMES DEAN, and THE JAMES DEAN ANNIVERSARY BOOK. These might be perceived by some as early biographies; however, one has to read with caution many of the articles contained in them. Nevertheless, the content addressed the issues most important to fans at the time: Was James Dean really dead? Did he commit suicide? What was he like as a person? Who were his friends? What did he do for relaxation and enjoyment? What do we know about his relationships? While there is at least some truth to most of the articles contained in these magazines, it wouldn't be long before all of these questions would be more fully discussed and in most cases, more completely exploited. While the published number of these magazines may seem large, collectors/fans will find each of these early items particularly difficult to obtain.

David Loehr, owner of the James Dean Gallery, which houses an extensive collection of James Dean memorabilia, asserts that there have been more than 400 magazines, from 16 different countries, in which articles about James Dean have appeared. American publications include: MODERN SCREEN, THE ROBB REPORT, HOLLYWOOD STUDIO MAGAZINE, SATURDAY REVIEW, ESQUIRE, NATIONAL ENQUIRER, JOURNAL OF POPULAR FILM, MOTION PICTURE, REDBOOK, PHOTOPLAY, COSMOPOLITAN, SEVENTEEN, and countless others. As varied as the list of magazine titles is, collectors will find an equally varied array of articles appearing in these magazines. Titles have included: "Jimmy's Happiest Moments," "Dean Ten Years After," "Jimmy's Last Message," "Rebel Without a Cause," "James Dean Tribute," "An Unforgettable Day with James Dean," "James Dean: His Life and Legend," and "Moody New Star." David Dalton's JAMES DEAN: THE MUTANT KING provides one of the best bibliographies from which to work as you begin to acquire published articles.

Perhaps the more unique and interesting group of magazines are those frequently referred to as "scandal" magazines. Their names alone—HUSH-HUSH, RAVE, INSIDE STORY, EXPOSED,

STRANGE, THE LOWDOWN, WHISPER, and CONFIDENTIAL—tell us about everything we might expect to find between their covers. These magazines, led by CONFIDENTIAL, provided readers with stories that most often approached the limits of slander, libel, and good taste. It was this same group that most frequently highlighted the distorted, strange, funny and controversial incidents in the star's life. From 1955 through 1958 there appeared 31 known "scandal" articles about James Dean. Included here were such masterpieces as: "James Dean's Torrid Love Letters", "Did Jimmy Dean Leave a Son?", "I was Jimmy Dean's Wife", "The Amazing James Dean Hoax!", "Jimmy Dean's Alive!", "James Dean: God of a Morbid Cult", and "James Dean Speaks from the Grave!" From a collectibles point of view, these articles are valuable because of the very real odd nature of most of them. The opportunity to obtain original issues of these magazines is rare indeed. Recently Shake Books (NY) published a collection of 19 of the best "scandal" articles, "The Best of James Dean in the 'Scandal' Magazines 1955-1958."

What is more striking though is that many of the so-called "scandal" articles have provided food for thought. This is to say, here are beginnings of many of the issues raised about Dean's life, most of which will be exploited in biographies.

The number of published biographies about James Dean is quite large. Beginning with the first in 1956, written by Dean's friend and college roommate at UCLA, Bill Bast, biographies appeared steadily with the more prosaic works of the 1970s followed by the more photographic-essay style of the 1980s.

In addition to the major works published in the United States during this period of time, there were also several biographies published in Germany, Great Britain, France, Italy, Spain, and Japan. Although most of the foreign works are translations of the American biographies, there have been several original works, which are often difficult to obtain, but are well worth the effort and the expense.

Careful examination of each biography reveals many differing interpretations of James Dean's life and career. What is even more striking is to discover how the same incidents have been instrumental in creating so many misconceptions about Dean, specifically with respect to his relationships on and off the movie set and his much debated and exploited sexual proclivities.

The most frequently sought after biography, and not surprisingly the most difficult to find, is William Bast's JAMES DEAN: A BIOGRAPHY (1956). This is perhaps the most personal of the biographies written. It is interesting to note that while the book includes Bast's own recollections about living with Jim and his impressions of him as both a friend and a person, several later biographers chose to reinterpret some of the same incidents.

It was during the period from 1974 through 1978 that most of the biographies appeared. This group provides the most representative view of James Dean. The books also established many of the misconceptions about Dean's life.

Venable Howard's JAMES DEAN: A SHORT LIFE (1974) presents the second most personal account of Dean. Perhaps this was because as one of the early biographers there was little to gain by creating "journalistic" misconceptions.

Following Howard's work were John Gilmore's THE REAL JAMES DEAN (1975) and Ron Martinetti's THE JAMES DEAN STORY (1975). Each of these works interprets incidents in James Dean's life differently, yet it is interesting how with each additional work, his life seems to acquire new and greater proportion and significance.

A truly remarkable biography, one that reflects tremendous research and reflection, is David Dalton's JAMES DEAN: THE MUTANT KING (1974). In this one book readers witness the metamorphosis of James Dean—from Jimmy, to Jim, to James. This biography holds the distinction of having created more true, devoted Dean fans than any other single work.

Two books re-issued during this period are John Howlett's JAMES DEAN: A BIOGRAPHY (1975) and Dennis Stock's JAMES DEAN REVISITED (1978). While Howlett's book provides little additional insight into the workings of James Dean, it does nonetheless read well. He is careful not to draw the unfounded conclusions reached by some previous authors. Stock's book is the first of several that approach Dean from a more pictorial perspective. Stock accompanied Dean to Fairmount Indiana, Dean's hometown, and did a series of photographs which were to appear later in a national magazine. While the article never materialized in the national magazine, many of these prints appear in JAMES DEAN REVISITED.

Stock's work established a direction that would become the dominating theme for several books published in the 1980s. While biographies of the 1970s sought to explore and question much of Dean's life, the works published in the 1980s provide extensive pictures of each stage of his complicated life and career.

For pictures three books come to mind immediately. David Dalton's JAMES DEAN: AMERICAN ICON (1984), Roy Schatt's JAMES DEAN PORTRAIT (1982), and Sanford Roth's JAMES DEAN (1983) each represent the extensively illustrated works of the 1980s. Stock, Shatt, and Roth were all friends of Dean's and their relationships with him are most clearly exhibited in the variety of photographs appearing in each of their works. Each book contains photography unique to the relationship of the author with Dean.

The aforementioned books stand out among the collectibles.

Other books are also of interest because of their unique character. While Dante's THE LAST JAMES DEAN BOOK would not rank as a must item, it nevertheless provides a series of vividly painted pictures of Dean in a variety of bizarre, almost morbid settings.

One controversy which blossomed after Dean's death was the question whether he committed suicide; the possibility he knew that he was to die. Many questioned whether he intentionally did not wear his seatbelt the day he was killed. All of these questions and many more are thoroughly and extensively researched, documented, and discussed in Warren Beath's THE DEATH OF JAMES DEAN (1986). This work not only provides extensive documentation about James Dean's death, it also contains rare, previously unpublished photography of the accident. The very topic of this book, and clearly, I believe the manner in which it is written, causes it to be unpopular among many devoted Dean fans.

Mick St. Michael's JAMES DEAN IN HIS OWN WORDS, a new publication and Randall Riese's THE DEAN DOCTRINE (forthcoming) are two works that will certainly be added to the list of collectible biographies currently sought by James Dean fans.

Foreign works which collectors might want to secure would certainly include: JAMES DEAN: THE FIRST AMERICAN TEENAGER (Japan, 1977), JIMMY DEAN CATALOGUE (Japan, 1977), JAMES DEAN:FOOTSTEPS OF A GIANT (Germany, 1986), THE FILMS OF JAMES DEAN (Great Britain, 1977), JAMES DEAN: A STORY IN WORDS AND PICTURES (Great Britain, 1985) JAMES DEAN STORY (France, 1975), JAMES DEAN IS NOT DEAD (Great Britain, 1984), and WISH YOU WERE HERE, JIMMY DEAN (Great Britain, 1989). In addition to these foreign works, there have been many editions of American biographies translated and published under foreign titles.

Magazines and books are the two largest groups of items to be found in the average James Dean collector's array of memorabilia. Other collectible items also appear from time to time in collections, especially in those of fans who began collecting when they were first licensed and manufactured in the late 1950s and early 1960s.

Steve Yeager's discography of James Dean is an excellent source when searching for the numerous 45s and albums that have appeared in tribute to James Dean. While many of the albums contain music from his movies, an occasional one provides songs about James Dean on the flip side. A particularly interesting album is The James Dean Story, with music from the movies and interviews with many of Dean's early Hollywood friends. This album is narrated by Steve Allen.

Three unique items, each appearing soon after Dean's death, include a mass-produced record, released by Romeo Records, and titled "James Dean on Conga Drums in an ad lib jam session..." This originally sold for $1.29 (mail order) and today commands in excess of $75. MODERN SCREEN magazine advertised and sold James Dean Medallions. These medallions today bring as much as $75 to $100. Perhaps because of the variety of masks available today (especially at Halloween), a life-size mask of James Dean, fashioned out of plastic that looked and felt like human flesh, doesn't seem to be such an odd collectible. Yet, in 1956 these masks were produced at the rate of two hundred a week by a Hollywood firm, and today such an item remains rare and would most certainly command record prices.

Along with the James Dean mask, several figures and busts have appeared. The most collectible bust, though, is the one commissioned by Dean himself in 1955. Only two weeks before his death, he had visited with Kenneth Kendall and asked him to do a bust of him. While small copies of this bust are readily available, larger models seem to meet more interesting fates. One bust placed on a monument to Dean in Park Cemetery in Fairmount Indiana was quickly stolen after its appearance there in 1957. More recently (October 28, 1988), Kenneth Kendall donated and unveiled a memorial to Dean at

Griffith Observatory. Atop this monument rests Kendall's bust of James Dean.

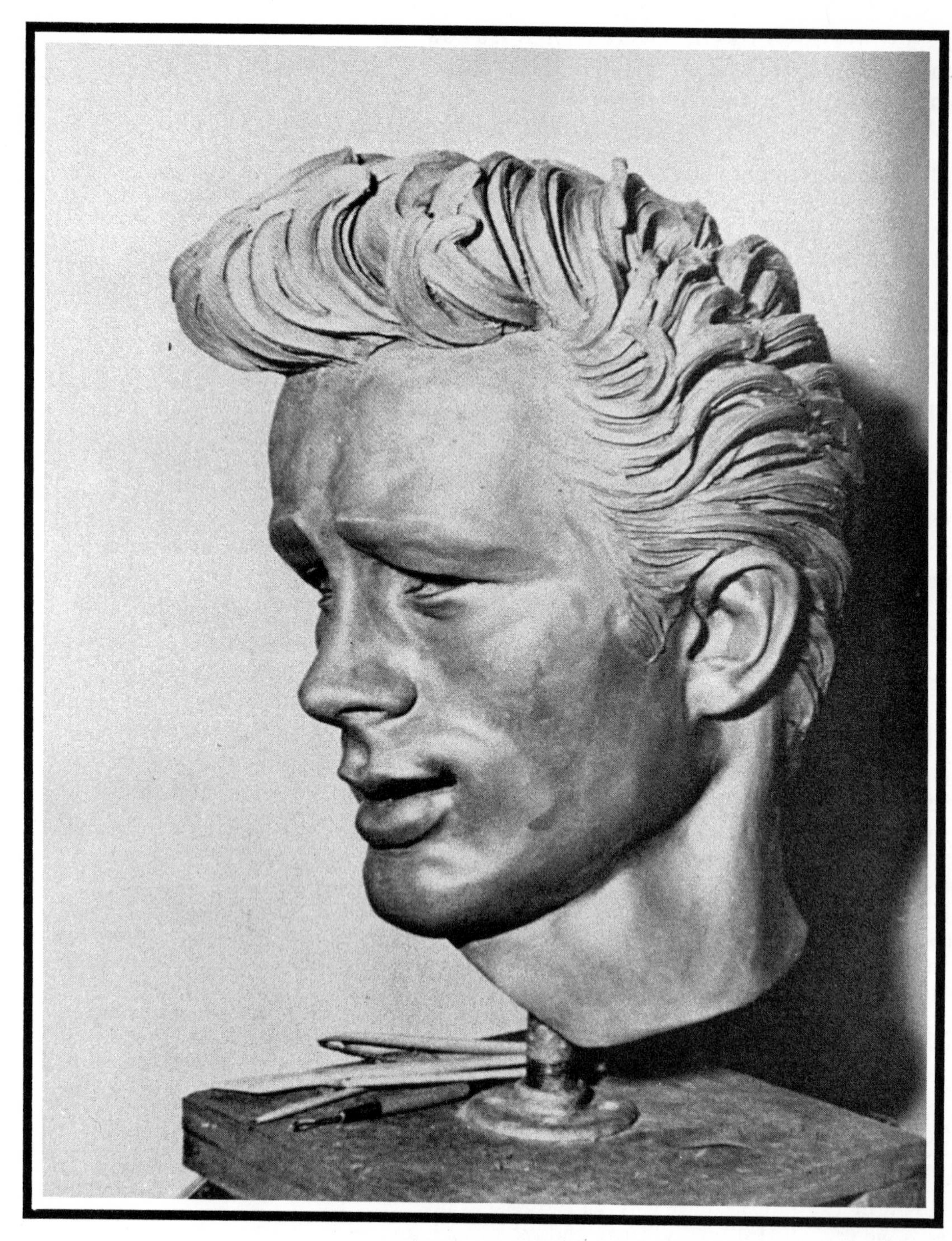

Movie memorabilia is surprisingly quite large, and it often commands the highest prices. Original movie posters, if in fair to good condition, can be expected to go for as much as $300 to $1000. While those of EAST OF EDEN and GIANT are more readily available, posters from REBEL WITHOUT A CAUSE remain the most prized and highly sought after movie item. Ed Knapp's "Those Thrilling Movie Lobby Posters" (ANTIQUES AND COLLECTING HOBBIES, September 1988) notes that "poster values vary depending on the name of the star featured. Extraordinary importance is attached to any poster material featuring such stars as...James Dean."

James Dean bust created by Kenneth Kendall.

In addition to the large, marquee-style movie posters, there are several lobby cards as well as smaller stills taken from the movies; these were often sent to theaters as advertisements. Another interesting movie-generated collectible was the set of life-size cut-outs of Dean, Taylor and Hudson produced for Warner Brothers and used to advertise the GIANT. Although this item now commands high figures, today there are many reproduced cut-outs from which to select. Some of these recent printings are life-sized while others are smaller versions of the originals.

While all of the items described previously are within the reach of a serious collector, several items remain only for the very lucky few, for whom money and persistence are limitless. These items, most of which were touched by Dean himself, either in life or death, according to Dalton "approach an almost idolatrous status, only equalled by the practice of reliquaries in the Middle Ages." Items included are personal belonging of Dean—athletic and racing trophies, school yearbooks, bongos, clothing, personal letters, books in which he inscribed messages, speeding tickets and family pictures. Fortunately, most of these items are safely displayed at the Fairmount Historical Museum, and others remain with Dean's relatives. How long such items will remain out of the hands of avid collectors remains to be seen.

Besides items personally belonging to Dean, collectors have been able to secure a variety of objects from actual movie sets. This list includes pieces of the Reata Mansion, fence posts, and the lariat used by Dean in GIANT as well as clothing and the tin toy monkey from REBEL WITHOUT A CAUSE. From time to time additional movie-related items appear only to be grabbed up quickly by a dedicated Dean fan.

While it seems only the very few, most of whom were personally acquainted with Dean, are lucky enough to possess personal items, one would question seriously the obsession of some to collect locks of hair, paint chips from his wrecked Porsche (which was displayed as a type of sideshow exhibit), rings set with broken glass from his car, chips from his headstone, and, finally the actual headstone, which disappeared soon after he was buried, and then reappeared some time later. Today the stone at his grave site is the one replaced after the first one disappeared. Obviously, these items are extremely valuable to someone, yet no real value can be placed on them. At least not with a clear conscience.

The immense popularity of James Dean after his death in 1955, and again in the late 1960s and early 1970s, seems to have provided collectors with a wealth of memorabilia to collect. Many earlier published books (in reprint editions), as well as re-issued posters, along with many new items, continue to provide additional objects for a Dean collection. Collectors still crave items relating to James Dean. It is perhaps in this vein that we can help the young "rebel" to continue to perpetuate a "cause". This cause clearly seems to be a reminder that there are indeed tangible manifestations (collectible items) available to each and every one of us that contribute to the development of JAMES DEAN THE LEGEND.

James Dean cut-outs and statues from the Enrico Perego collection.

Fans and Their Collections

It would be impossible to describe each fan's individual collection but when the membership of "We Remember Dean International" was asked to respond to an inquiry, several fans wrote back describing their collecting habits. Some collectors were teenagers when James Dean's movies were first released and remember his death, and the release of many memorabilia items for the first-time. Others only recently become interested in both James Dean and the world of memorabilia/collectibles associated with him. Some collections include a wide range of items while others consist only of books, or records, or magazines.

Many collectors strive to secure copies of the original movie posters and lobby cards. Novice collectors soon find that such items as movie posters and lobby cards are all too often out of the average collector's price range. Nevertheless, countless fans sent pictures of their rooms (many teenagers) which demonstrated a tremendous variety of newly released posters and reproductions of the original movie posters. It is obvious that for some fans items can only be original, while for the majority of fans, the reproduced items are acceptable. They permit the satisfaction of possessing James Dean collectibles while not commanding astronomical sums of money.

No matter which items you may choose to collect, it is wise to follow the examples set by Jayne Barnhart (Indiana); Jeanette Bostwick (Indiana); Gilly Savage (Massachusetts); Maxine Rowland (Ohio); Ken Grant (Missouri); John Howland (Kansas); Dorothy Peary (Illinois); Michael Pasley (Kansas); Larry Minor (Colorado); and Tricia Kelly (Illinois). Each has collected James Dean memorabilia purely for enjoyment. Unfortunately if James Dean memorabilia continues to command the incredible price increases of the recent past, the pleasure of collecting will diminish considerably. For now, while there are indeed very expensive items, the average collector of James Dean memorabilia can still find many excellent pieces to buy. Judging from experience, each of these items will become "items with a value" in the very near future.

James
DEAN

The Perego Collection

Enrico (Chicco) Perego shares his James Dean collection

Few people would argue about the extent to which James Dean has been able to conquer the affections of one generation after another since his untimely death in 1955. Yet, there are many who remain uncertain as to just how widespread Dean's popularity is today.

Clearly, his popularity is growing in the United States, but what seems to surprise most people is that Dean is every bit as popular in Japan, England, France, Italy and several other foreign countries. Dean is indeed worldwide.

Perhaps one of the best ways to assess the extent to which Dean's popularity has grown would be to examine many of the items which have been licensed and manufactured since his death. It seems only fitting as we examine the collectibility of James Dean memorabilia to take advantage of the opportunity to view illustrations of items from a truly unique collection of James Dean memorabilia. Unique, not only because of the size of the collection, but also because it happens to belong to an Italian gentleman who today resides in Milano, Italy.

Enrico (Chicco as his friends call him) Perego is 29 years old, lives in Milano, Italy and has been collecting James Dean memorabilia for 15 years. His collection consists of about 50 books, 200 magazines, 120 posters and a large collection of the more mundane items — pins, buttons, calendars, pencils, mugs, cups, plates, and many other mass-produced items.

Enrico purchased a pair of jeans in 1977. Along with the pair of jeans he received a free poster of James Dean which he promptly took home and hung on his wall. Soon friends saw the poster on the wall and made plans. For his birthday they gave him an Italian edition of John Howlett's JAMES DEAN A BIOGRAPHY. Enrico, like so many others, was hooked.

From this point on he began to search for each item that he could find. His friends also continued to find items for him.

In 1985 he made his first trip to the United States. He visited Los Angeles. During this trip he rented a car and drove to Cholame to visit the monument. It was during this trip that he managed to buy two suitcases full of Dean items.

In 1986 Enrico again came to the United States. This time he visited New York and then rented a car and drove to Fairmount, where he spent three days visiting with the Winslows. He again added numerous items to his ever-increasing collection.

Enrico travels a great deal throughout Europe. He has been able to add many items from several different European countries.

Today Enrico continues to add to his collection. He is also a member of "We Remember Dean International", "The James Dean Fan Club", and "Dean Downunder".

The variety of items included in these photographs of Enrico's collection typifies what most collectors have or would like to have.

TOP:
Italian movie posters
a) EAST OF EDEN,
b) REBEL WITHOUT A CAUSE, c) GIANT.

RIGHT:
Dean buttons.

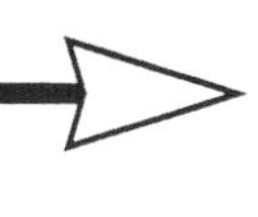

JAMES DEAN BUTTONS

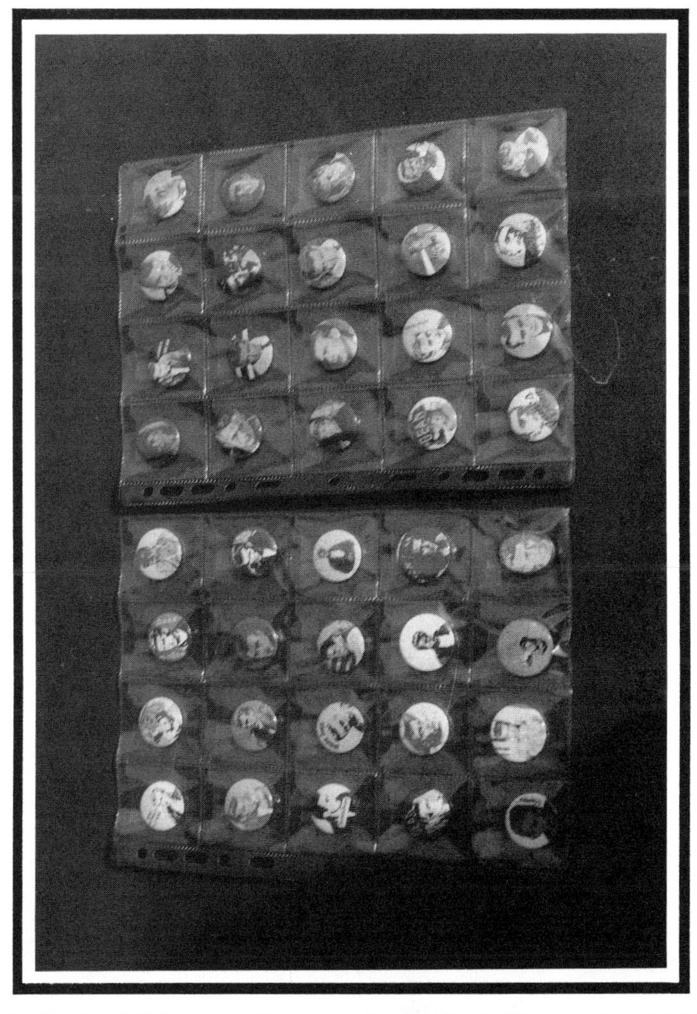

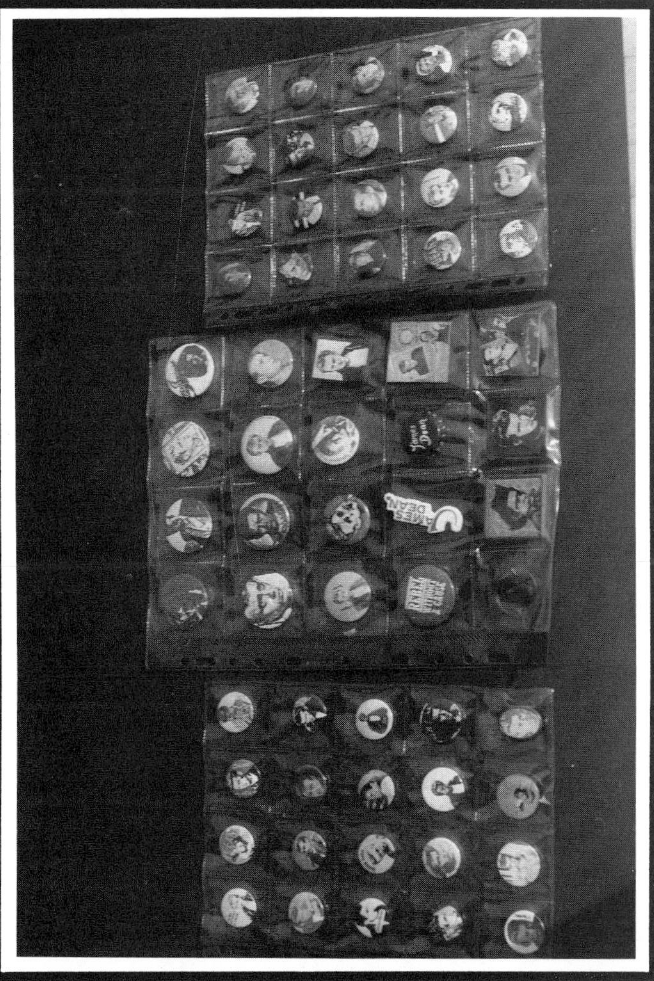

EPOCA
EPOCA
IL MIO AMICO JAMES DEAN
CINÉ REVUE
JAMES DEAN

NOVELLA
cleo
JAMES DEAN
SEPTEMBER 30 1955 NEVER HAPPENED

SCREEN LEGENDS
EVA
THE BEST OF JAMES DEAN
IN THE "SCANDAL MAGAZINES" 1955–1958
INCLUDES:
Did James Dean Really Die?
James Dean's Black Madonna
James Dean's Torrid Love Letters
Did Jimmy Dean Leave A Son?
I Was Jimmy Dean's Wife!
Plus 16 Others Exactly As Originally Printed!
Exclusive! Amazing! Fully Illustrated! Possibly True!

JIMMY DEAN
RETURNS
Jimmy's own scrapbook!
JAMES DEAN
15 PICTURES! NEW STORIES
THE STRANGE MYSTERY
HOW HE LIVED
HOW HE LOVED
JAMES DEAN non è MORTO
DM9,80
LA VITA DEL GRANDE ATTORE IN UN APPASSIONANTE RACCONTO
Lire 100

OPPOSITE PAGE:
***TOP LEFT:** Italian and French magazines.*
***TOP RIGHT:** A variety of magazines with feature articles on Dean.*
***BOTTOM LEFT:** THE BEST OF JAMES DEAN IN THE SCANDAL MAGS alongside several magazines.*
***BOTTOM RIGHT:** Assorted magazines featuring James Dean.*

JAMES DEAN MAGAZINES

THIS PAGE:
A collection of magazines featuring James Dean.

THIS PAGE:
TOP: German biography (left), Howlett's THE REAL JAMES DEAN (center), Portuguese biography (right).
BOTTOM LEFT: Japanese, German and Italian biographies.
BOTTOM RIGHT: Japanese biographies, plus a Greek biography of Dean.

OPPOSITE PAGE:
TOP LEFT: French and English biographies; TOP RIGHT: Early edition American biographies.

BOTTOM LEFT: Japanese and English biographies; BOTTOM RIGHT: The extrememly rare Morrissey's JAMES DEAN IS NOT DEAD, the almost equally rare Dante's THE LAST JAMES DEAN BOOK and a German Dean book.

JAMES DEAN BOOKS

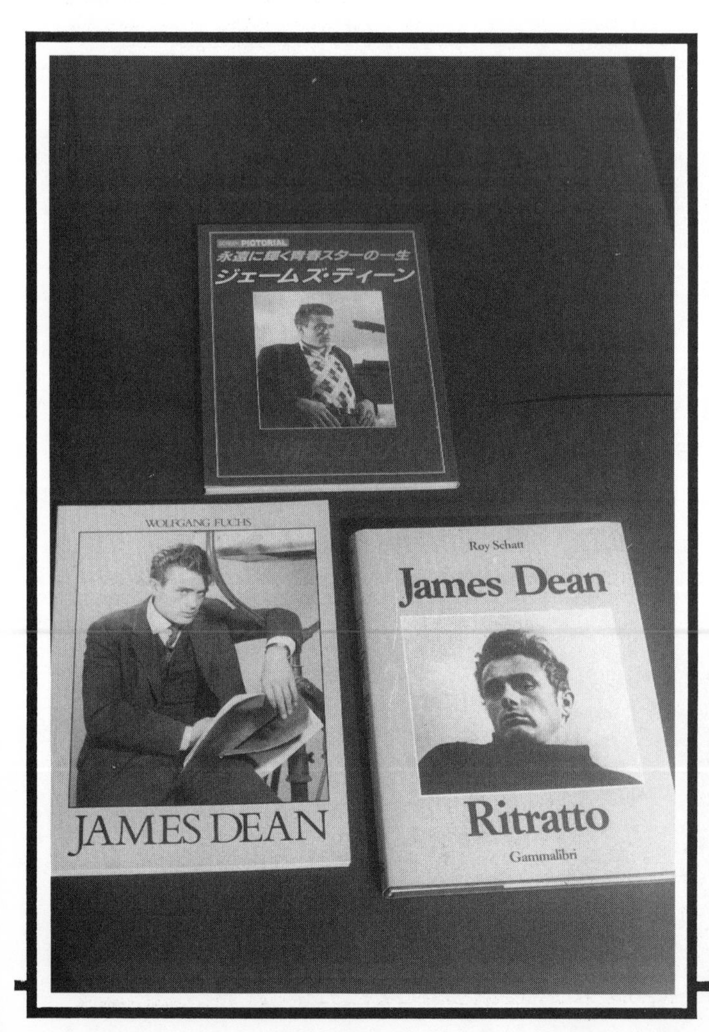

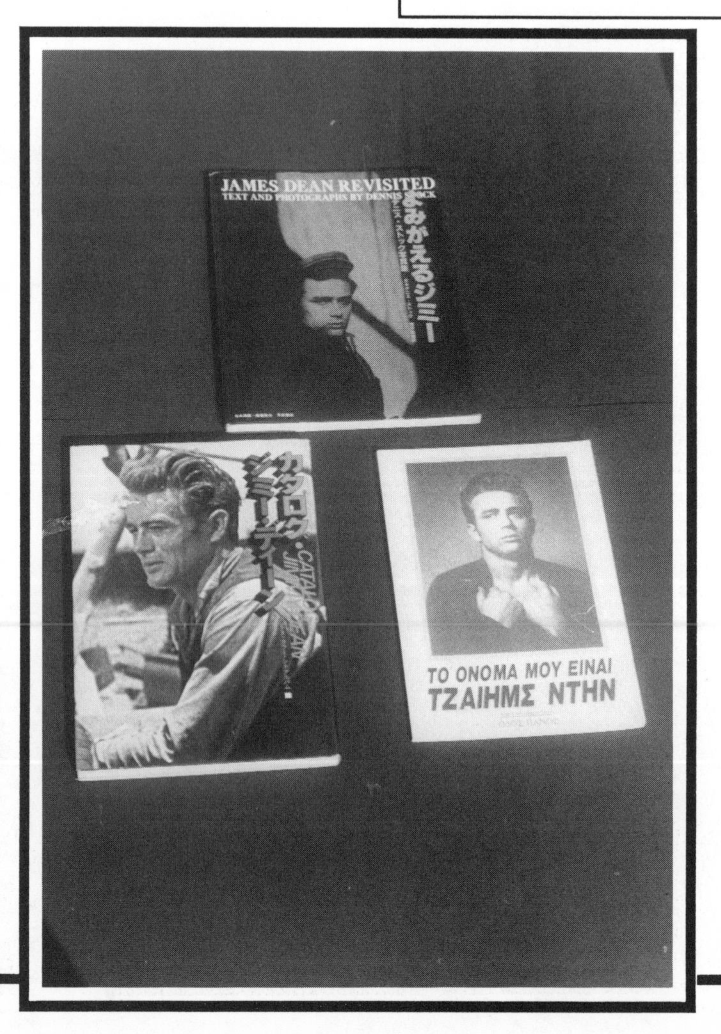

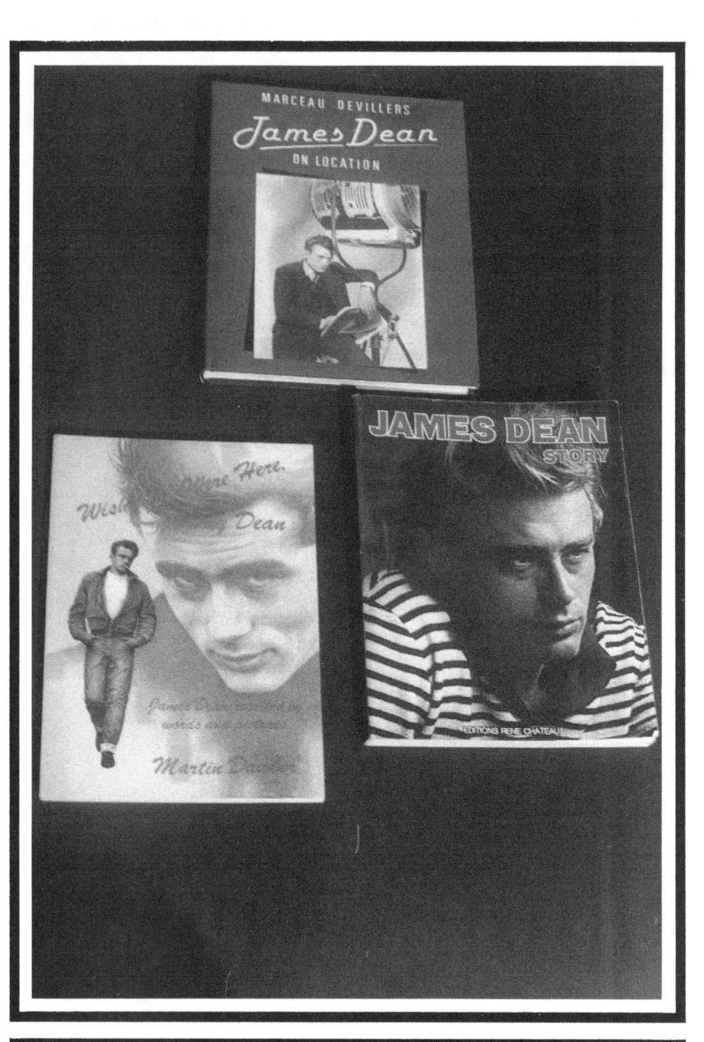
MARCEAU DEVILLERS
James Dean
ON LOCATION
JAMES DEAN
STORY
EDITIONS RENE CHATEAU
Martin Dawber

JAMES DEAN
A SHORT LIFE
James Dean
JAMES
DEAN
RONALD MARTINETTI
DIE JAMES DEAN STORY

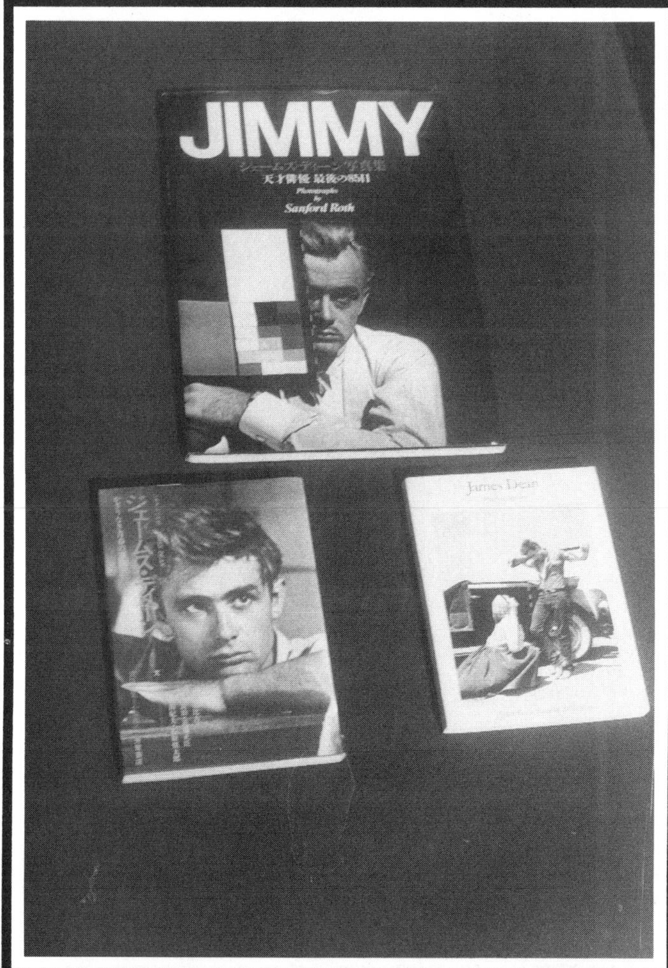
JIMMY
Photographs by Sanford Roth
James Dean

JAMES DEAN
Not Dead
by Morrissey
THE LAST
JAMES DEAN
BOOK
BY DANTE
JAMES DEAN
EIN PORTRÄT

JAMES DEAN
THE MUTANT KING
DAVID DALTON

James Dean
JOHN HOWLETT
James Dean
JAMES DEAN
青春よ永遠に
JAMES DEAN

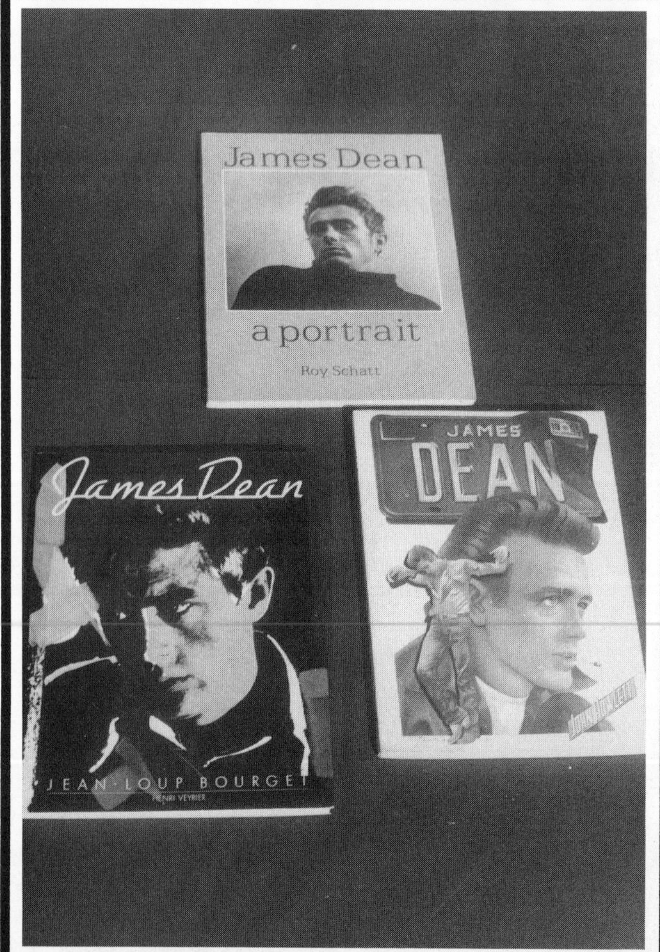
James Dean
a portrait
Roy Schatt
JAMES
DEAN
James Dean
JEAN-LOUP BOURGET
HENRI VEYRIER
JOHN HOWLETT

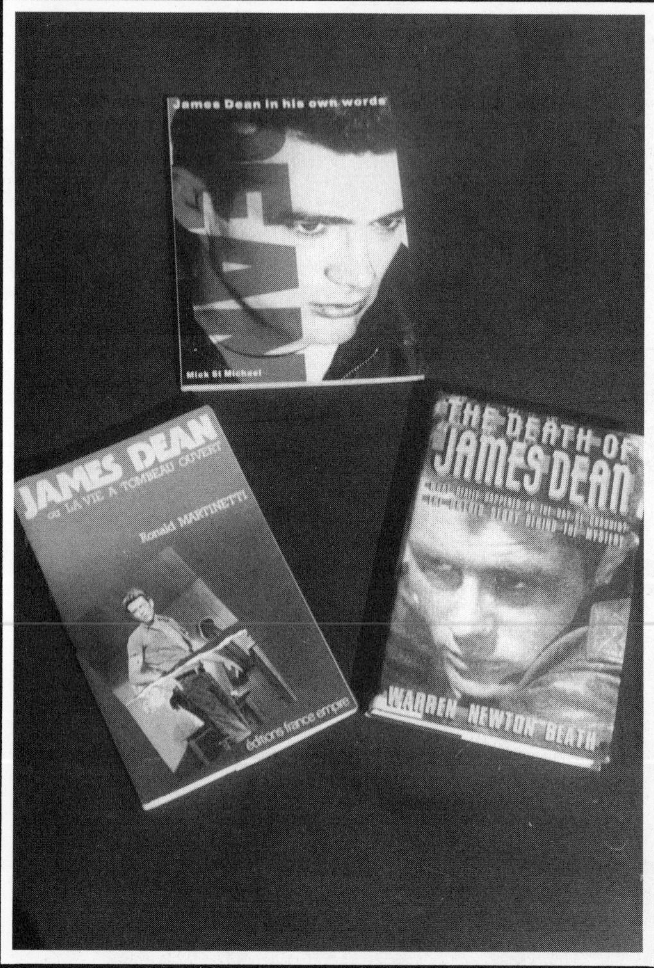
James Dean in his own words
Mick St Michael
JAMES DEAN
ou LA VIE A TOMBEAU OUVERT
Ronald MARTINETTI
éditions france empire
THE DEATH OF
JAMES DEAN
WARREN NEWTON BEATH

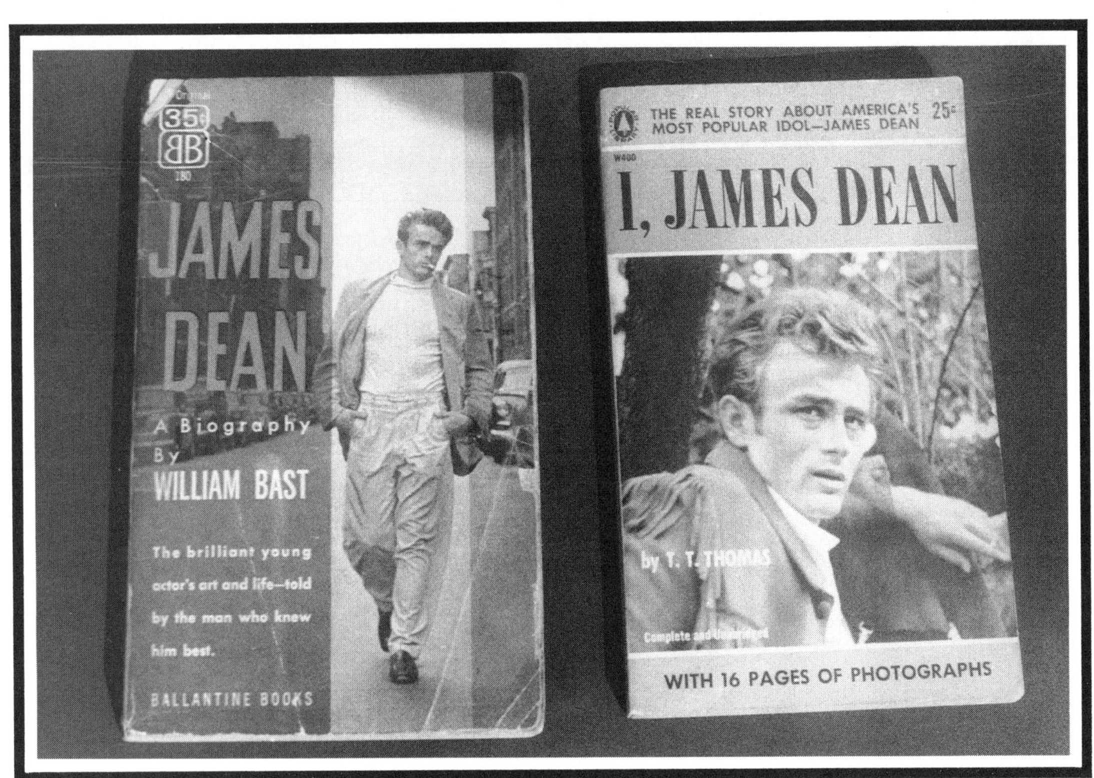

OPPOSITE PAGE: TOP LEFT: Dalton's JAMES DEAN THE MUTANT KING TOP RIGHT: German and Japanese biographies along with Roth's JAMES DEAN. BOTTOM LEFT: Dean biographies. BOTTOM RIGHT: The recent JAMES DEAN IN HIS OWN WORDS and a French edition of Ronald Martinetti's JAMES DEAN STORY.

THIS PAGE: TOP: The first biographies— Bast's book from 1956, written by Dean's friend (left) and Thomas's 1957 biography (right). BOTTOM: Books featuring excellent photographs of Dean's life and work.

JAMES DEAN BOOKS

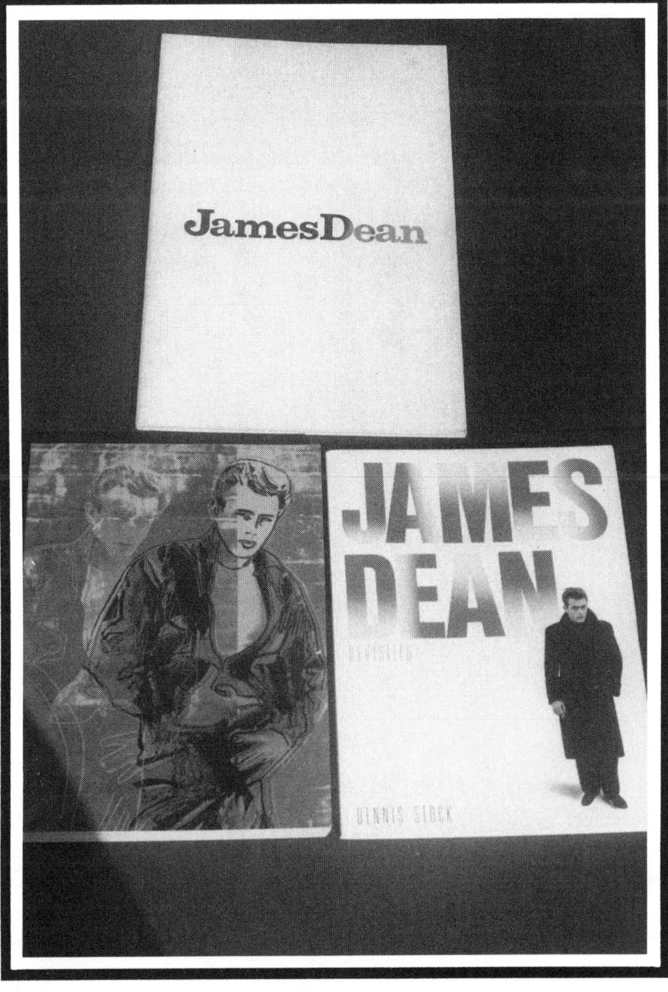

JAMES DEAN CALENDARS

JAMES DEAN VIDEOS

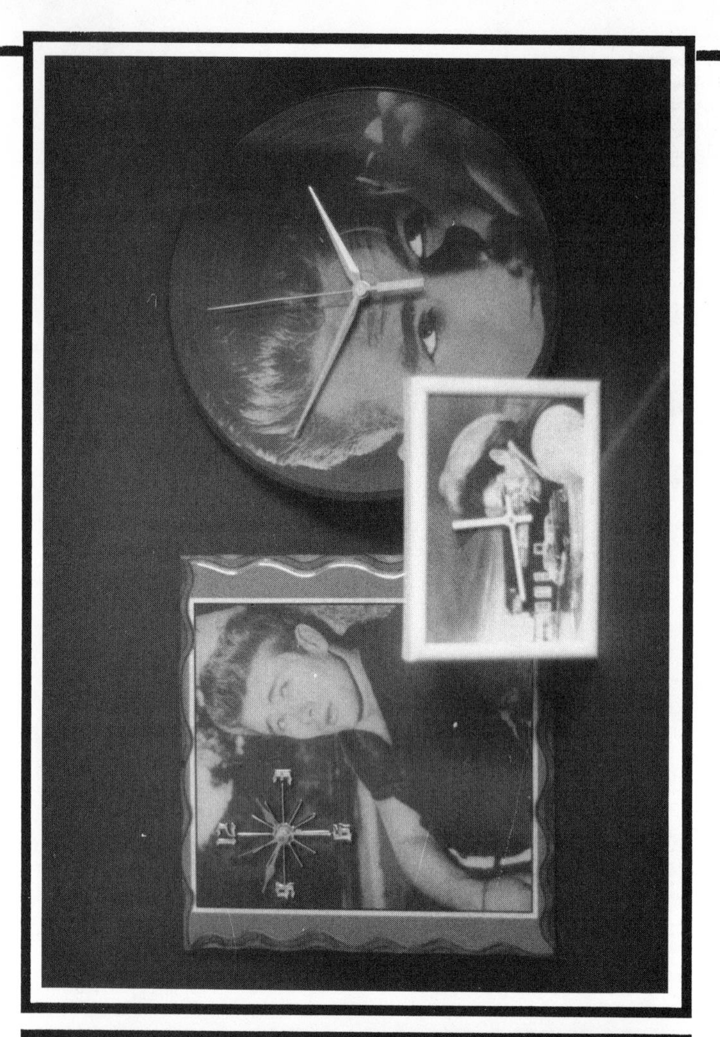

James Dean
12
9
3
6

EAST OF EDEN
A L'EST D'EDEN

James Dean
DEAN
poster book
JAMES DEAN
DIARY
JAMES DEAN
JD

***TOP:** Photo albums containing extremely rare pictures of Dean.*

***BOTTOM:** Photos, postcards and magazines.*

JAMES DEAN PHOTOS

***OPPOSITE PAGE:** Clocks, postcards, poster and postcard books.*

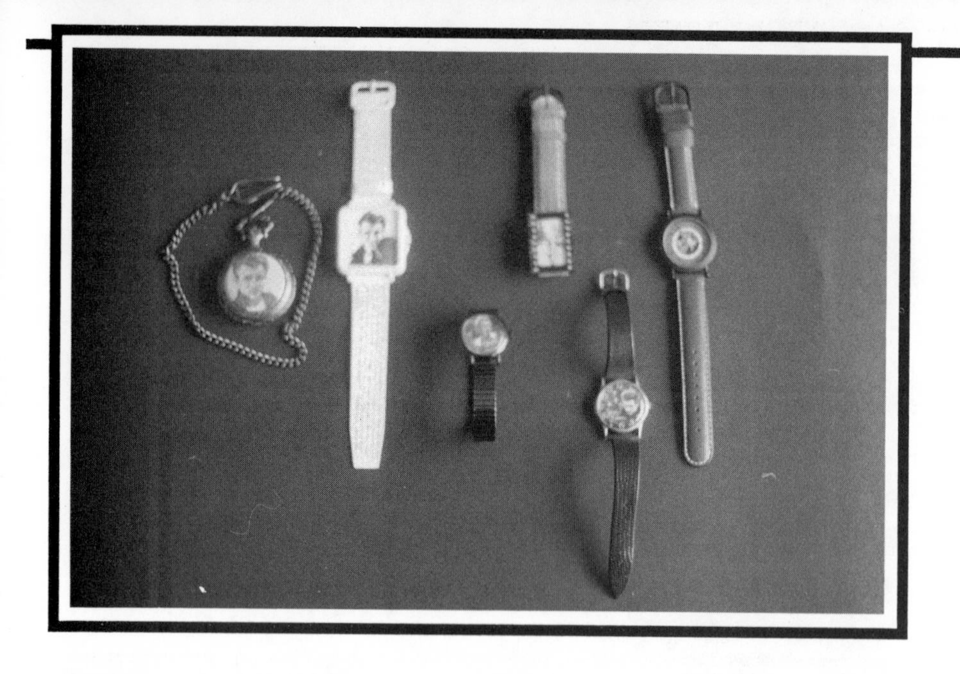

THIS PAGE:

TOP: Watches

MIDDLE: Jeans, an early item that was marketed.

BOTTOM: License plate, ashtray and other memorabilia.

OPPOSITE PAGE:

TOP: Stand-ups and statues

MIDDLE: License plate and key rings

BOTTOM: Stickers

JAMES DEAN MERCHANDISE

WHEN HE DIED, A LEGEND WAS BORN.
James Dean
He lived fast.
Died young.
And shaped the style
of a whole generation.
Now a new generation
has its chance to see...
Rebel
Without a Cause
'AA'
JAMES DEAN in "REBEL WITHOUT A CAUSE" AA Also Starring NATALIE WOOD with SAL MINEO / JIM BACKUS / ANN LORAN / COREY ALLEN / WILLIAM HOPPE
Screenplay by STEWART STERN · Produced by DAVID WISEBART · Directed by NICHOLAS RAY · Music by LEONARD ROSEMAN
CINEMASCOPE / WARNER COLOUR From Warner Bros. A Warner Communications Company · Released by Columbia-Warner Distributors

James Dean Video Specialist

Robert Rees has during the last few years been able to secure what appears to be the largest collection of video material available on James Dean. His collection includes movies, rare television appearances, and numerous documentary and short clip materials about James Dean. It is indeed unfortunate that much of this material is unavailable to the average collector. Rees himself points out that materials on James Dean are becoming harder and harder to acquire.

Most materials carried by small label companies are marketed only for a short period of time. Dean fans are fortunate to have a person as knowledgeable as Robert Rees when it comes to collecting and preserving for the future rare materials about James Dean. Fans who would like more information about James Dean video materials might wish to write Bob at: 21334 Park Mount Drive - Katy, Texas 77450.

Rees' collection, far more extensive than is indicated here, includes the following:

JAMES DEAN REMEMBERED (ABC 1974 Lawford special with Mineo/Sammy Davis/Steve Allen/Natalie Wood/Leonard Rosenman); 1985 Cable News Network coverage; SHOWBIZ TODAY clip; ENTERTAINMENT TONIGHT clip; PM MAGAZINE 1979; TODAY SHOW 1980; WORLD OF PEOPLE 1980; HOLLYWOOD CLOSEUP 1983; JAMES DEAN AN AMERICAN ORIGINAL; THE LEGACY; Dean Impersonator, PM MAGAZINE; "Teenage American" (hosted by John Ritter, May 1986); TV coverage (NBC ,CBS, ABC) November 1, 1988 LIFE MAGAZINE TRIBUTE, November 1986; Steve Allen documentary on James Dean; home movie videos which include a fan's trip from Los Angeles to Cholame, Marfa Texas, and the ruins of Reata. TV appearances include: "10,000 Horses Singing"; "The Evil Within"; "Long Time Till Dawn"; "Hill Number One"; "Asleep on Guard"; "The Harvest"; "Bells of Cockaigne"; "The Unlighted Road"; and "I am a Fool".; Dean Los Angeles Sites, 1989; Dean Fairmount Sites, 1989; "Lost Dean TV Shows" Current Affair, September 27, 1989; Come Back to the Five and Dime, Jimmy Dean, Jimmy Dean; James Dean: Portrait of a Friend; 9/30/55; Bit parts in "Has Anybody Seen My Gal?"; "Sailor Beware"; and "Fixed Bayonets"

Please bear in mind that this listing serves only to highlight the extensive array of television video materials which have appeared since Dean's death.

Fans clamor to join an early club—
The James Dean Fan Club!

James Dean Fan Clubs

The fans we meet,
the friends we
make
the love in all our
hearts,
Jimmy directing
this final act
with us playing all
the parts,
The man, his
dreams we share
each month
in our club
WRDI.
What is essential
is indeed
invisible to the
eye.
— Ken Grant
(Missouri)

Fan clubs come and go. For one reason or another clubs fade away almost as quickly as they develop. Immediately following Dean's death according to Dalton in JAMES DEAN, AMERICAN ICON, "in the absence of an official fan club many hundreds of local organizations were set up all over the States, some of which were amalgamated to form the larger of the Dean fan clubs: 'Dedicated Deans' had a membership of 430,600; 'Dean's Teens' 392,450; 'Lest We Forget' 376,870; the 'James Dean Memorial Club' 328,590."

While fan clubs offered members a varying degree of solace in knowing there were many who were also suffering over the loss of James Dean, members of such clubs could, at least for paying membership dues, expect to receive a glossy print suitable for framing, numerous studio stills, including some which would be wallet size, and a membership card. Most wished at least to provide a forum through which members could bind together in order to perpetuate the memory of a great actor, James Dean. While such items are important to new fans, today's fans seem to demand more significant items from their clubs, namely a newsletter and an opportunity to get together and share memories and stories about their "star".

In an effort to provide readers with a number of fan clubs from which to select should they wish to belong to a fan club, an effort was made to contact each club for which there was currently an address available. Unfortunately, like so many fan clubs, there were some which have long since ceased to exist. Some others, for one reason or another, chose not to respond to requests.

Addresses and membership information have been provided for those clubs which responded to a request for information. It would seem that those clubs which offer the most to their membership are the most likely to exist for an extended period of time. One can also observe that it appears to be the membership that largely perpetuates both the spirit of James Dean and the spirit of the club.

Sylvia Bongiovanni, co-founder of "We Remember Dean International", provides us with much insight about the formation of a club, and more importantly, about what it takes to produce a newsletter for club members. The existence of a club newsletter seems critical to the survival of a fan club. And judging from the quality of newsletter "We Remember Dean International" members receive, it is also no surprise that "WRDI" remains one of the most successful James Dean fan clubs.

It goes without saying that the contributions made by James Dean fan clubs to the creation and perpetuation of the James Dean legend are as varied as the membership of these clubs. However, what seems unique to each is their dedication to James Dean.

James Dean Fan Clubs

WE REMEMBER DEAN INTERNATIONAL

WE REMEMBER DEAN INTERNATIONAL

c/o Sylvia Bongiovanni, P.O. Box 5025, Fullerton, California 92635

WE REMEMBER DEAN INTERNATIONAL, originally, "We Remember Dean" was founded in 1978 for the purpose of putting James Dean fans in touch with one another and to share thoughts and feelings about this very special actor.

The goal of WRDI is to preserve the memory of James Dean, while providing the members with a network to share both information and their thoughts about Jimmy. The membership is constantly increasing. The participation of the members is outstanding. That is one of the reasons for the success of WRDI.

WRDI provides a bimonthly newsletter (for a time this newsletter was monthly). It informs its members of new books, magazines, audio and videotapes, current events, and so on. It also profiles its members. Most importantly, the Club Newsletters represent a convergence of ideas and emotions, a source of friendship between fans.

The Club has been a major factor in getting fans together, and different events take place within the membership; get-togethers at someone's home; a yearly James Dean Walking Tour in New York; a gathering in Fairmount each September 30, the anniversary of Jim's death.

This kind of dedication and structure seem required to provide fans with an opportunity to remain truly respectful to both the memory of James Dean and to their club.

Sylvia Bongiovanni, on a more personal note, recalls vividly how she came to be personally involved in the formation of WE REMEMBER DEAN INTERNATIONAL:

"I've been a fan of Mr. Dean's since the 1950s, first seeing him on television shows such as the G.E. THEATRE and SCHLITZ PLAYHOUSE. When EAST OF EDEN opened in New York my friend and I went to see Jimmy in it. He appealed to me in a way no other actor had done; his movements were so articulate. He had a face you just wanted to scrutinize. He showed such sensitivity you really felt for him. He was magnetic. After reading David Dalton's THE MUTANT KING in the mid-1970s, I wrote the Fairmount Museum in Indiana (Jim's hometown) to see if they had James Dean memorabilia for sale. The secretary, Helen Kirkpatrick, replied and thus started our correspondence. With Mrs. Kirkpatrick's assistance, a registry book was placed in the Museum so fans could write one another. Mrs. Kirkpatrick began sending me the names from the registry. I started to write these fans from various states, and within a year was writing about 20 or so fans. This was in 1977 and 1978. Then in the

Spring of 1978, Mr. Bill Lewis wrote me, and we decided to form a club for James Dean—thus it all began.

While writing DEANMANIA I felt it was important not only to include information about fan clubs, but because they have played such an important part in the creation of James Dean The Legend, I determined that information related to the actual formation of a club was perhaps equally important in order to assess the extent to which clubs and their fans perpetuate the spirit and memory of James Dean.

Sylvia Bongiovanni was very kind to spend time considering questions which I posed to her. Sylvia's responses to these questions allow us not only to understand the contribution fan clubs can and do make to the creation and perpetuation of a legend, but most importantly, demonstrate the degree of dedication many fans have for James Dean.

We began with such basic information as when the WRDI was formed and how many people belong.

"WRDI was started in July of 1978," Sylvia explained. "Currently (1990) we have a membership of 500.

"WRDI has members in about 48 states. Abroad we have members in about 30 different countries, and Canada. Their ages vary with the youngest being about 12 and the oldest about 65. Their occupations vary—we have lawyers, housewives, students, secretaries, teachers, professors, doctors, construction workers, a variety. I'd say that the male/female ratio is about evenly divided."

I asked her to recall some of the earliest activities that the club sponsored.

She enthusiastically enumerated them, obviously enjoying the memories. "Early activities sponsored by the club included luncheons in Fairmount, Indiana in September and a get-together around Jimmy's birthday at a member's home." A major step the club undertook was launching the newsletter. Sylvia explained, "The club was organized in July of '78. The idea for a newsletter came in about September or October of that year when I received my bimonthly newsletter from the Johnny Mathis Club! I had joined the Mathis Club many years before with a free membership form in one of his record albums. In the fall of '78, when I received my Mathis Newsletter, I then realized 'this is what I have to do with the Dean Club' and in November of 1978 our first WRDI Newsletter was issued. One page, one side. It didn't contain too much in the beginning and ran maybe one to two pages. As the membership grew and I became more knowledgeable about what to do, the Newsletter contained more articles and information. It was sent monthly until about one year ago (it is now bimonthly), and now contains at least 12 pages. We've had club members design our master Newsletter—Sherry Hauser and Norman Petterson.

"I keep all newsletter items and articles in a folder, and thank goodness the folder is constantly full! Putting it together in draft after draft form is time-consuming; knowing what to put in and what to leave for the next issue is difficult. I have an electric typewriter only and so I don't use a memory for my drafts; and there are times when

I retype one page perhaps two or three times. "(Organizing the material) is the most difficult task. I'm fairly well organized but when you're finally doing an issue there's a heck of a lot of notes!

"I write, edit, publish and distribute the Newsletter single-handedly, Sylvia continued. "I now have my mother helping with putting the Newsletter in the envelope and stamping them. With her helping me now, it has cut down on this part of my work. To produce one issue from beginning to end (end meaning delivery to the post office) takes about 25 hours. Doing the Newsletters bimonthly has helped me. It gives me more free time to attend to other club matters. In a way I prefer it sent monthly because it would be more timely, but bimonthly is just as informative if not more so as I now include more pages."

I asked her to recall which newsletters she was most proud of. She responded, "I'm actually proud of all the newsletters. Each one contains different information and articles. The participation of the membership in sending me items and articles is outstanding. In the past couple of years we've had issues dedicated to honorary members on their birthdays and these issues are always special."

Since there have been many James Dean Fan Clubs, many of which lived only briefly, I asked her to explain what makes WRDI unique. Why has it continued to grow and distinguish itself as one of the best clubs to honor James Dean. Sylvia said, "I think what makes WRDI unique is the friendliness and caring of its members. They care about James Dean and care about their club. I can count on just about anyone to help when needed, to advise when needed and to be there for me. I've tried to maintain an informal club, getting the members to correspond with one another, and indeed they have. Members who did not know each other previously are now friends. There's a special bond now and I think the members are the reason for the growth and success of the club. I work hard at our club, a couple of hours each day, I would guess, which has to be done to maintain the club. There is a lot of love and hard work in what I do and my rewards are great — friends.

"The Newsletters and the club have greatly contributed to the memory and spirit of James Dean in that he has sparked in each one of us a special kinship to one another. Many good things have come out of us from being fans and we all want to see that he is remembered for years to come."

Each year the club publishes highlights of the year relevant to James Dean and the fandom he created. I requested she note three or four of the highlights that stood out in her mind as important. She listed, "The Griffith Observatory Dedication; The James Dean Gallery; and The Cinemax special 'Forever James Dean' in which members participated."

Considering all the work Sylvia does for the club, I asked what benefits she personally derived and of what she was most proud. She said, "I'm most proud of the club and its members. I'm proud of the mutual respect we have for one another and the respect that is given to James Dean. I've made friends that are true and lasting. I've had the privilege of meeting Jim's family and friends in Fairmount, and some of his associates in California and New York.

"The benefits I've derived from the club? There are many—friendship, a better knowledge of James Dean, a wonderful collection, and sharing with others."

I asked her to imagine that James Dean could come back and what his response would be to "We Remember Dean International"?

"I think he would be glad to know how his fans feel about him; he would be glad to know he has brought people together; and I think he'd come to our get-togethers and enjoy his fans."

"James Dean may be the mirror of my dream,
Or a clear reflection in a stream,
But the shadows of his past,
I'll remember until the day I die.
And his laughter and his tears,
I'll make my souvenirs."
— Sarah King, England

Other Clubs And Organizations

JAMES DEAN MEMORIAL FOUNDATION

The James Dean Memorial Foundation was established in May of 1956. It is not really a club. Marcus Winslow, Jim's uncle, recalls that with all the money being sent to Warner Brothers "it was from these donations that the idea came about for the James Dean Memorial Foundation. Fans sent money for 'some kind of memorial,' but a statue in the park or monument in the cemetery wouldn't be right: 'Jimmy wouldn't have liked a statue. He'd have ducked his head and rubbed the back of his neck and said, 'Aw, not for me, Marc. That's not for me'".

The JAMES DEAN MEMORIAL FOUNDATION was established with the following specific objectives in mind:

1. To act as a living and perpetual memorial to James Dean; 2. To operate exclusively in the furtherance of the dramatic, musical, and literary arts and sciences; 3. To encourage and promote education in these fields by providing scholarships, fellowships, or other financial assistance; 4. To provide educational facilities and instruction in these fields; 5. To encourage achievement in these fields by the presentation of awards, cash prizes and other tokens of recognition; 6. To promote and encourage public knowledge and support of the theatre arts and sciences; 7. To make gifts and benefactions to such organizations as shall from time to time be determined as deserving by the Board of Directors and Board of Advisors; 8. To render needed financial assistance to proven and deserving young professional talents as shall be determined by the two boards.

THE JAMES DEAN FAN CLUB

Greg Larbes, Director/Editor, 3924 St. John's Terrace, Cincinnati, Ohio 45236

THE JAMES DEAN FAN CLUB seems to fit the description that most would give when asked to define a fan club. Members receive an 8x10 B&W picture of James Dean and a picture of Ann Doren and Jim together in a scene from REBEL. In addition, they receive a bimonthly newsletter which typically contains trivia, poetry, art, and information on publications and hard-to-find items connected with James Dean. A percentage of dues from this club goes to purchase flowers to be placed on Dean's grave each year.

Recent newsletters included information about Dean's appeal in Japan; the discovery of Dean's 1955 motorcycle; the impending wrecking of James Dean's high school; and several newsclippings about stars from Dean movies, including Julie Harris and Dennis Hopper.

JAMES DEAN MEMORY CLUB

497 ATLANTIC AVE., BROOKLYN, NEW YORK 11217. Unfortunately the JAMES DEAN MEMORY CLUB did not respond to requests for information about their club.

DEAN DOWNUNDER

c/o DEB RANCE, 35 CUTHBERT ST., HEATHMONT, VICTORIA, AUSTRALIA 3135

DEAN DOWNUNDER is perhaps the most recently established fan club. Begun in May 1989 by Deb Rance, this club will attest to the growing interest in James Dean in Australia.

The Legend Lives On...

In the preface to this book I stated that it was my intent to present as complete and accurate a picture of James Dean THE MAN, THE CHARACTER and THE LEGEND as I possibly could. Now as I reflect about the development of this book, I can't help but wish that I had the opportunity to include much more. It seems as though each time I finished one section, something or somebody created in me an urge to go back and tell you more. I fought this urge many times while deciding what to include and what not to include. To be complete and accurate is I found very difficult. I realize now that there will be somebody who will find an inaccuracy and no doubt someone will establish that I was not as complete as I could have been in the treatment of a movie, or in the listing of memorabilia. So be it. I believe what I have set forth here in DEANMANIA is a true representation of James Dean The Person, The Character and The Legend.

I too, like David Dalton in THE MUTANT KING have come to realize that "despite pilgrimages, fan clubs, revered relics, biographies, and communications with the departed Dean, we ultimately have to accept that we will never know Jimmy. The further we get from his time, the more frozen he becomes, the more impossible it becomes to extract him from his myth. More and more, we receive the myth of James Dean as the most complete, consumable story..."

For 35 years now we have attempted to understand James Dean The Person and James Dean The Character. In the process of our attempting to do this we have created James Dean The Legend. It seems likely that the legend which has been created will not die soon. As long as there are devoted James Dean fans there will always be Dean-Mania; as long as there are teenagers there will always be James Dean THE MAN; as long as there are movies there will always be James Dean THE CHARACTER; and as long as these elements are present there will always be James Dean THE LEGEND.

Further Reading...

The research for this book began by reading and re-reading much of the documented material about James Dean, his life and career. While many of the books cited below are no longer available, it seemed important to include each, particularly because the total demonstrates the extent to which Dean's life and career have been documented.

Bast, William. James Dean A Biography. New York: Ballantine Books, 1956.

Considine, David. The Cinema of Adolescence. North Caroline: McFarland, 1987.

Dalton, David. James Dean The Mutant King. New York: St. Martin's Press, 1974.

————. James Dean American Icon. New York: St. Martin's Press, 1984.

Dawber, Martin. Wish You Were Here Jimmy Dean James Dean Recalled in Words and Pictures. London: Columbus Books, 1988.

Fuchs, Wolfgang J. James Dean Footsteps of a Giant. Berlin: TACO, 1986.

Gilmore, John. The Real James Dean. New York: Pyramid Books, 1975.

Herndon, Venable. James Dean: A Short Life. New York: Doubleday and Company, 1974.

Howlett, John. James Dean: A Biography. London: Plexus, 1975.

Martinetti, Ron. The James Dean Story. New York: Pinnacle Books, 1975.

Morella, Joe and Edward Epstein. Rebels: The Rebel Hero in Film. Secaucus New Jersey: Citadel Press, 1983.

Morin, Edgar. The Stars. New York: Grove Press, 1960.

Schatt, Roy. James Dean: A Portrait. New York: Delilah Books, 1982.

In addition to the sources cited above, much information was gathered from the hundreds of articles which have appeared detailing practically every aspect of James Dean's life. These articles have appeared in such publications as Hollywood Studio Magazine; Screenplay; Photoplay; Modern Screen, Cinemonde, Hollywood Reporter, New York Times, Variety, Movie Life, Screen Stories, Time, as well as in numerous scandal magazines, specifically: Whisper, Rave, Exposed, Inside Story, Hush-Hush, Confidential and Lowdown.

Finally, interviews with many people far more knowledgeable than I about James Dean and materials/documents sent to me by James Dean fans helped to fill gaps in the public record.

The Films Of Elvis: The Magic Lives On
Written by Hal Schuster
The legend of the King of Rock and Roll lives on, twelve years after his death. Long live the King! His name, of course, is Elvis Presley, and while his unprecedented musical accomplishments and personal endeavors have been well chronicled in the past, people remain unaware of his startlingly successful film career. During the 13 years between 1956 and 1969, Elvis starred in 31 films, running the gamut from cornball musical to serious drama. Now, Pioneer presents THE FILMS OF ELVIS: THE MAGIC LIVES ON, a comprehensive guide to the King's films, providing reproductions of theatrical posters, a breakdown of the songs performed in each movie, complete cast listings and a critical analysis of all 31 motion pictures. Jam-packed with never before published photos!
$14.95..........164 pages
Color Cover, Black and White Interior Photographs
ISBN#1-55698-223-2

THE FILMS OF ELVIS

- Love Me Tender (1956)
- Loving You (1957)
- Jailhouse Rock (1957)
- King Creole (1958)
- G.I. Blues (1960)
- Flaming Star (1960)
- Wild in the Country (1961)
- Blue Hawaii (1961)
- Follow That Dream (1961)
- Kid Galahad (1962)
- Girls! Girls! Girls! (1962)
- It Happened at the World's Fair (1963)
- Fun in Acapulco (1963)
- Viva Las Vegas (1963)
- Kissin' Cousins (1964)
- Roustabout (1964)
- Girl Happy (1964)
- Tickle Me (1965)
- Harum Scarum (1965)
- Paradise, Hawaiian Style (1965)
- Frankie and Johnny (1965)
- Spinout (1966)
- Double Trouble (1966)
- Easy Come, Easy Go (1967)
- Clambake (1967)
- Stay Away, Joe (1968)
- Speedway (1968)
- Live a Little, Love a Little (1968)
- Charro! (1969)
- The Trouble With Girls (1969)
- A Change of Habit (1969)

Paul Mccartney: 20 Years On His Own
Written by Edward Gross
Paul McCartney is in the midst of a world tour that is shattering records, and continues to establish him as a force to be reckoned with in the music industry, a point emphasized on August 29, 1989 when 200,000 tickets to nine performances sold out in less than half an hour.
PAUL MCCARTNEY: 20 YEARS ON HIS OWN looks at the life of Paul McCartney from the time the Beatles went their separate ways in 1970 to the press conference announcing his FLOWERS IN THE DIRT world tour, including his struggles to reach stardom a second time, his triumphant world tour in 1976, his 1980 drug bust in Japan, and his reaction to the death of John Lennon.
This volume is a loving tribute to an entertainment dynamo whose music has touched the imagination of millions for nearly three decades.
$9.95...........100 pages
Color Cover, B &W Interior Photos
ISBN#1-55698-263-1

Secret File: The Unofficial Making Of A Wiseguy Written by Edward Gross
Innovative. Intelligent. Unpredictable.
These words come to mind when discussing WISEGUY, the show currently revolutionizing the television medium while gathering one of the strongest cult followings to greet a network series in many years.
SECRET FILE: THE UNOFFICIAL MAKING OF A WISEGUY goes behind the scenes of this explosive series, profiling star Ken Wahl, presenting conversations with co-stars Jonathan Banks and Jim Byrnes, and interviewing the producers, writers, directors and guest stars. Also including an in-depth episode guide to the first two seasons and profiles of every villain that has come up against Organized Crime Bureau agent Vincent Terranova.
$14.95.............140 pages
Color Cover, Black and White Interior Photos
ISBN#1-55698-256-9

The Secret Of Michael J. Fox's Success Written by Edward Gross
•FAMILY TIES was the number two rated television series for most of its run
•BACK TO THE FUTURE was the highest grossing film of 1985
•Fox's films have grossed nearly half a billion dollars!
THE SECRET OF MICHAEL J. FOX'S SUCCESS looks at the career of this multi-faceted actor, examining his early days of struggle, life on FAMILY TIES and the making of each of his films. The text also provides critical analysis of each of his roles and reveals his unique appeal.
$14.95..........164 pages
Color Cover, Black and White Interior Photos
ISBN#1-55698-232-1

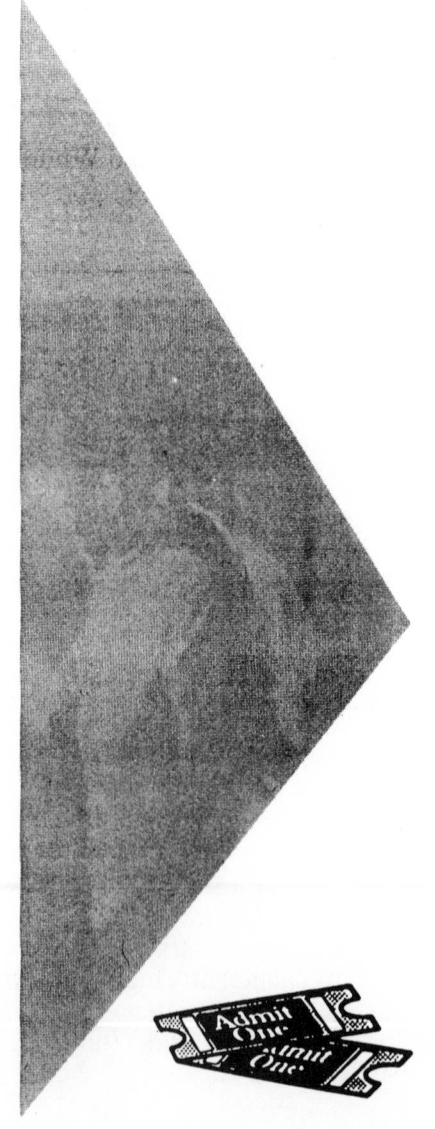

Boring, But Necessary Ordering Information!

Payment:

All orders must be prepaid by check or money order. Do not send cash. All payments must be made in US funds only.

Shipping:

We offer several methods of shipment for our product. Sometimes a book can be delayed if we are temporarily out of stock. You should note on your order whether you prefer us to ship the book as soon as available or send you a merchandise credit good for other goodies or send you your money back immediately.

Postage is as follows:
Normal Post Office: For books priced under $10.00—for the first book add $2.50. For each additional book under $10.00 add $1.00. (This is per indidividual book priced under $10.00. Not the order total.)
For books priced over $10.00—for the first book add $3.25. For each additional book over $10.00 add $2.00.(This is per individual book priced over $10.00, not the order total.)
These orders are filled as quickly as possible. Shipments normally take 2 or 3 weeks, but allow up to 12 weeks for delivery.
Special UPS 2 Day Blue Label Rush Service or Priority Mail(Our Choice). Special service is available for desperate Couch Potatoes. These books are shipped within 24 hours of when we receive the order and should normally take 2 to 3 days to get from us to you.
For the first RUSH SERVICE book under $10.00 add $5.00. For each additional 1 book under $10.00 add $1.75. (This is per individual book priced under $10.00, not the order total.)
For the first RUSH SERVICE book over $10.00 add $7.00 For each additional book over $10.00 add $4.00 per book.(This is per individual book priced over $10.00, not the order total.)

Canadian shipping rates add 20% to the postage total.
Foreign shipping rates add 50% to the postage total.
All Canadian and foreign orders are shipped either book or printed matter.
Rush Service is not available.

DISCOUNTS!DISCOUNTS!

Because your orders keep us in business we offer a discount to people that buy a lot of our books as our way of saying thanks. On orders over $25,00 we give a 5% discount. On orders over $50.00 we give a 10% discount. On orders over $100.00 we give a 15% discount. On orders over over $150.00 we giver a 20 % discount.

Please list alternates when possible.

Please state if you wish a refund or for us to backorder an item if it is not in stock.

100% satisfaction guaranteed.

We value your support. You will receive a full refund as long as the copy of the book you are not happy with is received back by us in reasonable condition. No questions asked, except we would like to know how we failed you. Refunds and credits are given as soon as we receive back the item you do not want.

Please have mercy on Phyllis and carefully fill out this form in the neatest way you can. Remember, she has to read a lot of them every day and she wants to get it right and keep you happy! You may use a duplicate of this order blank as long as it is clear. Please don't forget to include payment! And remember, we love repeat friends.

COUPON PAGE

________Secret File: The Unofficial Making Of A Wiseguy $14.95 ISBN # 1-55698-256-9
________Number Six: The Prisoner Book $14.95 ISBN# 1-55698-158-9
________Gerry Anderson: Supermarionation $14.95
________Calling Tracy $14.95 ISBN# 1-55698-241-0
________How To Draw Art For Comicbooks: Lessons From The Masters
ISBN# 1-55698-254-2
________The 25th Anniversary Odd Couple Companion $12.95 ISBN# 1-55698-224-0
________Growing up in The Sixties: The wonder Years $14.95 ISBN #1-55698-258-5
________Batmania $14.95 ISBN# 1-55698-252-6
________The Year Of The Bat $14.95
________The King Comic Heroes $14.95
________Its A Bird, Its A Plane $14.95 ISBN# 1-55698-201-1
________The Green Hornet Book $14.95
________The Green Hornet Book $16.95 Edition
________The Unofficial Tale Of Beauty And The Beast $14.95 ISBN# 1-55698-261-5
________Monsterland Fear Book $14.95
________Nightmare On Elm Street: The Freddy Krueger Story $14.95
________Robocop $16.95
________The Aliens Story $14.95
________The Dark Shadows Tribute Book $14.95 ISBN#1-55698-234-8
________Stephen King & Clive Barker: An Illustrated Guide $14.95 ISBN#1-55698-253-4
________Drug Wars: America fights Back $9.95 ISBN#1-55698-259-3
________The Films Of Elvis: The Magic Lives On $14.95 ISBN#1-55698-223-2
________Paul McCartney: 20 Years On His Own $9.95 ISBN#1-55698-263-1
________Fists Of Fury: The Films Of Bruce Lee $14.95 ISBN# 1-55698-233-X
________The Secret Of Michael F Fox $14.95 ISBN# 1-55698-232-1
________The Films Of Eddie Murphy $14.95 ISBN# 1-55698-230-5
________The Lost In Space Tribute Book $14.95 ISBN# 1-55698-226-7
________The Lost In Space Technical Manual $14.95
________Doctor Who: The Pertwee Years $19.95 ISBN#1-55698-212-7
________Doctor Who: The Baker Years $19.95 ISBN# 1-55698-147-3
________The Doctor Who Encyclopedia: The Baker Years $19.95 ISBN# 1-55698-160-0
________The Doctor And The Enterprise $9.95 ISBN# 1-55698-218-6
________The Phantom Serials $16.95
________Batman Serials $16.95